CHINESE
C·O·O·K·I·N·G

GOLDEN APPLE PUBLISHERS

CHINESE COOKING

A GOLDEN APPLE PUBLICATION/
PUBLISHED BY ARRANGEMENT WITH OTTENHEIMER PUBLISHERS INC.

JUNE 1986

GOLDEN APPLE IS A TRADEMARK OF GOLDEN APPLE PUBLISHERS

ALL RIGHTS RESERVED
COPYRIGHT © 1986 BY OTTENHEIMER PUBLISHERS, INC.

THIS BOOK MAY NOT BE REPRODUCED IN WHOLE OR IN PART,
BY MIMEOGRAPH OR ANY OTHER MEANS WITHOUT PERMISSION.
For Information Address: GOLDEN APPLE PUBLISHERS,
666 FIFTH AVENUE, NEW YORK, N.Y. 10103

ISBN 0-553-19860-2

Contents

Appetizers	5
Soups and Salads	13
Poultry Main Courses	26
Fish and Seafood Main Courses	48
Meat Main Courses	61
Rice and Noodles	78
Vegetables	82
Desserts	87
Equivalent Measures	94
Index	95

Appetizers

Sweet-and-Sour Spareribs

5 tablespoons soy sauce	1 tablespoon cornstarch
2 tablespoons sherry	1 tablespoon vinegar
2 cloves garlic, minced	1 teaspoon cornstarch
1 teaspoon sugar	Oil for cooking
1½ pounds spareribs	

Combine 3 tablespoons soy sauce, 1 tablespoon sherry, garlic, and 1 teaspoon sugar; blend well.

Have butcher cut crosswise through bones of spareribs at about 1- to 1-1/2-inch intervals. Cut bones apart. Pour soy-sauce mixture over spareribs. Let stand at room temperature 1 hour; stir occasionally. Blend in 1 tablespoon cornstarch.

Blend 2 tablespoons sugar, 2 tablespoons soy sauce, 1 tablespoon sherry, vinegar, and 1 teaspoon cornstarch together in saucepan. Cook over medium heat, stirring constantly, until thickened. Set aside.

Heat approximately 3 inches oil in deep pot. Drain marinade from spareribs. Add a portion of the meat at a time to hot oil; cook until well browned. Drain on paper towels. Place cooked spareribs in cooked sauce; coat well. Cover and chill. Serve spareribs at room temperature. Makes about 24 to 28 pieces.

6/Appetizers

Chicken Wings

1 **(10-ounce) bottle soy sauce**	⅓ **cup brown sugar**
2 **teaspoons gingerroot, freshly grated**	1 **teaspoon dark mustard**
	24 **chicken wings**
2 **cloves garlic, minced**	**Garlic powder**

Mix soy sauce, ginger, garlic, brown sugar, and mustard together; blend well. Marinate chicken in mixture 2 hours or longer. Drain wings; reserve marinade. Bake 1-1/2 hours at 350°F, turning and basting with marinade frequently. Sprinkle with garlic powder.

Place under broiler a minute or two to get crispy, just before serving. Makes 8 to 12 servings.

Chicken Wings in Oyster Sauce

3 **tablespoons oil**	2 **tablespoons soy sauce**
2 **cloves garlic, crushed**	3 **tablespoons oyster sauce**
8 **chicken wings, each divided into 3 parts**	1 **tablespoon sugar**
	½ **cup water**

Preheat wok. Coat bottom and sides with oil. Rub bottom and sides with garlic; discard garlic. Add middles and tips of wings; brown on both sides. Add rest of wing pieces and brown them.

Mix soy sauce and oyster sauce together; stir into chicken. Stir in sugar and water. Cover wok; cook over medium-low heat 15 minutes. Makes 4 servings.

Crusty-Crumbed Chicken Wings

1 **pound chicken wings**	¼ **teaspoon pepper**
¼ **cup oil**	¼ **teaspoon oregano**
1 **cup bread crumbs**	2 **teaspoons curry powder**
½ **teaspoon salt**	

Disjoint chicken wings into 3 pieces. Put aside wing tips to use for future soup stock. Brush wing pieces with oil.

Combine bread crumbs, salt, pepper, oregano, and curry powder in a plastic bag. Add 6 pieces of chicken at a time; shake well to coat evenly. Place chicken in large baking dish. Continue shaking a few pieces at a time until all chicken is well coated.

Bake chicken at 400°F for 35 minutes or until chicken is crusty outside and tender inside. Serve this appetizer with your favorite Chinese duck sauce. Makes 6 servings.

Crusty-Crumbed Chicken Wings

Cucumber Hors d'Oeuvres

2	tablespoons oil	1	teaspoon soy sauce
3	small red chili peppers, seeded and cut into very thin slices	2	tablespoons sugar
		¼	teaspoon salt
		1	tablespoon vinegar
4	medium to large cucumbers, cut into 2-inch lengths, quartered, and seeded		

Heat oil in skillet. Add chili peppers; stir-fry 4 seconds. Add cucumbers; stir-fry 30 seconds. Add soy sauce, sugar, and salt; stir until well blended.

Refrigerate at least 24 hours. Remove cucumbers from liquid and sprinkle with vinegar. Makes 6 servings.

8/Appetizers

Egg Rolls

Dough
½ **pound flour**
1½ **cups water**
Salt
1½ **teaspoons peanut oil**

Filling
½ **pound green cabbage**
1 **leek**
1 **medium-sized onion**
1 **(8-ounce) can bamboo**
  shoots
1 **(4-ounce) can mushrooms**

4 **tablespoons oil**
4 **ounces ground beef**
4 **ounces ground pork**
2 **cups fresh bean sprouts**
4 **tablespoons soy sauce**
2 **tablespoons sherry**
Salt
Cayenne pepper

Peanut oil
Beaten egg yolks
6 **cups oil for deep frying**

Place flour in bowl. Slowly stir in water, making sure that you always stir in the same direction. Add salt and 1-1/2 teaspoons peanut oil and cover bowl. Let rest for 30 minutes.

Meanwhile, prepare filling. Wash and drain cabbage and leek and cut into thin slices. Chop onion. Drain bamboo shoots and cut into fine strips. Drain and coarsely chop mushrooms. In skillet, heat 4 tablespoons oil and add ground meats; cook until lightly browned. Stir in cabbage, leek, onion, and bamboo shoots. Cook for 5 minutes. Add mushrooms and bean sprouts and cook for an additional 2 minutes. Season to taste with soy sauce, sherry, salt, and cayenne pepper. Remove from heat and set aside.

Brush an 8-inch skillet with peanut oil. Pour in 1/8 of the egg roll dough; tilt skillet to spread batter evenly. Over low heat, cook until set. Turn out onto moistened paper towels. Cover with another moistened paper towel. Continue until all dough is used up.

Cut egg roll rounds into 6-inch squares. Divide filling among the 8 egg rolls. Fold 2 opposite corners of egg rolls toward middle. Starting with corner closest to you, roll up egg roll. Brush inside of opposite corner with small amount of beaten egg yolk; seal egg roll.

Heat oil in deep frying pan. Add rolls and fry until done. Put paper towels on cake rack; place egg rolls on rack and drain. Keep them warm and serve on preheated platter. Makes 8 egg rolls.

Egg Rolls

Wontons

- ½ pound pork, minced
- ¼ cup fresh mushrooms, minced
- 1 tablespoon scallion, minced
- ¼ teaspoon salt
- ⅛ teaspoon freshly ground black pepper
- 1 egg yolk
- Wonton squares
- Peanut oil

Mix minced pork, mushrooms, and scallion with salt, pepper, and egg yolk. Place 1/2 teaspoonful of the mixture in center of wonton square. Fold one corner up over filling at an angle to make 2 askew triangles. Pull bottom corners of triangles gently down below their base. Overlap tips of the two corners slightly and pinch them together.

Fry in hot peanut oil and drain. Serve with Chinese mustard or catsup mixed with a little horseradish. Makes approximately 120 wontons.

10/Appetizers

Pineapple Cocktail Barbecue

1	can pineapple chunks (approximately 16 ounces), drained; reserve syrup	1	stick cinnamon
		1	teaspoon salt
		1	teaspoon cornstarch
1	jar red-cherry preserves or jelly (approximately 10 ounces)	2	teaspoons water
		1	tablespoon soy sauce
		1	pound ground chuck made into cooked meatballs
¼	cup catsup		
3	whole cloves		

Combine pineapple syrup with cherry preserves, catsup, cloves, cinnamon, and salt. Heat to boiling. Dissolve cornstarch in water until it makes smooth paste. Stir into boiling sauce. Cook until cornstarch thickens and turns clear.

Add pineapple chunks and soy sauce. Pour over meatballs. Keep warm in chafing dish. Serve with toothpicks. Makes 6 to 8 servings.

Shrimp Toast

¼	teaspoon sesame-seed oil	8	slices 2-day-old, thinly sliced white bread
¼	teaspoon soy sauce		
Pinch of white pepper		1	quart vegetable oil
Pinch of salt			
½	pound uncooked shrimp, cleaned and deveined		

Add sesame-seed oil, soy sauce, pepper, and salt to shrimp; mix thoroughly. Cut 32 rounds from bread slices. Spread shrimp mixture evenly on 16 rounds. Top each circle with another round; press edges together.

Heat oil in deep pot until very hot. Drop each round into oil; turn to brown evenly. Takes approximately 2 minutes. Drain on paper towels. Makes 16 pieces.

Honan-Style Scallops

1	cup soy sauce	2	tablespoons sugar
1	tablespoon lemon juice	¼	teaspoon MSG (optional)
2	teaspoons fresh gingerroot, finely chopped	1	pound scallops, cut into bite-sized pieces

Combine soy sauce, lemon juice, ginger, sugar, and MSG (if used) in large saucepan; bring to boil. Add scallops; cook over medium-high heat until all liquid has evaporated. Makes approximately 25 appetizers.

Appetizers/11

Spareribs in Honey Sauce

3 pounds pork spareribs	Salt and pepper
3 tablespoons oil	1 level tablespoon prepared
1 large onion, chopped	mustard
1 clove garlic, crushed	4 tablespoons soy sauce
2 tablespoons lemon juice	1 cup white stock or water
4 tablespoons orange juice	and chicken stock cube
2 tablespoons honey	

Cut spareribs into individual ribs or ask your butcher to do this for you. Place ribs in a roasting pan.

Heat oil in a saucepan and fry onion and garlic until softened but not browned. Stir in all remaining ingredients and bring to a boil. Pour sauce over ribs and cook in a 325°F oven for 1-1/2 hours, basting frequently. Drain off the sauce and serve hot. Makes 4 to 6 servings.

Cocktail Meatballs

1 (20-ounce) can pineapple chunks	1 teaspoon salt
	1 teaspoon cornstarch
1 jar red cherry jelly or preserves	1 tablespoon soy sauce
	1 pound ground chuck
¼ cup catsup	made into cooked
3 whole cloves	meatballs
1 stick cinnamon	

Drain pineapple and reserve juice. Combine juice with jelly or preserves, catsup, cloves, cinnamon, and salt. Heat to boiling. Dissolve cornstarch in enough liquid (either water or a small amount of the pineapple-juice mixture) to make a smooth paste and stir into the boiling mixture. Cook until cornstarch thickens and clears.

Add pineapple chunks and soy sauce. Pour over cooked meatballs in a chafing dish and serve warm. Makes about 4 servings.

Sweet-and-Sour Plum Sauce

½ cup water	2 tablespoons catsup
1 cup plum jelly	2 tablespoons vinegar

Place ingredients in saucepan and stir. Bring to boil. Serve warm. Makes approximately 1-1/2 cups sauce.

12/Appetizers

Mandarin-Orange Gelatin

Sweet-and-Sour Sauce

4 tablespoons catsup	2 tablespoons cornstarch dissolved in ½ cup cold water
¼ cup brown sugar	
2 tablespoons soy sauce	
3 tablespoons wine vinegar	
2 tablespoons dry white wine	

Combine catsup, sugar, soy sauce, vinegar, and wine in saucepan. Bring to a boil. Add the cornstarch dissolved in water to sauce. Cook over low heat, stirring constantly, until sauce has thickened. Makes about 1-1/4 cups sauce.

Soups and Salads

Honan-Style Chicken Salad

1	pound chicken meat, shredded (leftover chicken is fine)	2	tablespoons soy sauce
		2	tablespoons red-wine vinegar
3	cucumbers, cut into matchstick pieces	2	tablespoons sugar
		1	teaspoon crushed red pepper
1	leek, white part only, cut into small thin pieces	1	tablespoon sesame oil
1	tablespoon fresh gingerroot, minced	1	tablespoon sesame seeds, toasted in hot frying pan

Mix chicken with cucumbers; place in serving dish. Sprinkle with leek and gingerroot; chill in refrigerator.

Mix soy sauce, vinegar, sugar, red pepper, and oil together; blend thoroughly. Stir in sesame seeds. Just before serving, toss with chicken mixture. Makes about 4 servings.

14/Soups and Salads

Lychee and Sesame Salad

5 to 6 lettuce leaves or
  Chinese cabbage
5 tablespoons oil
3 tablespoons vinegar
3 level tablespoons sesame
   seeds, toasted
1 level teaspoon brown sugar
1 teaspoon soy sauce
¼ level teaspoon dry mustard

Salt and pepper
1 (5-ounce) can water
   chestnuts, sliced
½ can bean sprouts (about ½
   pound), drained and
   rinsed
4 spring onions, sliced
1 can lychees

Wash lettuce leaves and place in refrigerator to crisp. Combine oil, vinegar, sesame seeds, sugar, soy sauce, mustard, and salt and pepper to taste in a large serving bowl. Add water chestnuts, bean sprouts, spring onions, and lychees. Shred lettuce into the bowl and toss together lightly. Serve at once. Makes 4 to 6 servings.

Mandarin-Orange Gelatin

1 (11-ounce) can mandarin
   oranges, drained; reserve
   ½ cup liquid
3 tablespoons sauterne
2 (3-ounce) packages
   orange-flavored gelatin

1 envelope unflavored
   gelatin
2 cups hot water
1 cup cold water

Combine oranges with 2 tablespoons sauterne.

Combine orange-flavored and unflavored gelatin in large bowl; mix well. Add hot water; stir until gelatin is dissolved. Stir in 1 tablespoon sauterne, reserved mandarin-orange liquid, and cold water. Chill until gelatin is thick and syrupy.

Pour about 1/2 cup gelatin into 1-1/2-quart mold rinsed in cold water. Arrange orange segments petal-fashion in gelatin. Chill until set.

Spoon about 1-inch layer thickened gelatin over oranges. Arrange layer of orange segments around edge of mold. Chill until set. Spoon another layer of gelatin over oranges. Repeat layers. Chill until set. Makes 6 servings.

Lychee and Sesame Salad

Soups and Salads/15

16/Soups and Salads

Mandarin Salad

1 teaspoon soy sauce	¼ cup sweet pickle relish
¼ cup French dressing	¾ cup mayonnaise
2 cups diced cooked veal (ham can be substituted)	½ teaspoon salt
¼ cup onion, chopped	Dash of freshly ground black pepper
2 cups fresh bean sprouts	

Combine soy sauce and French dressing. Marinate veal in mixture 45 minutes; chill. Add remaining ingredients; toss lightly. Serve on bed of lettuce. Makes 4 servings.

Fruited Rice Salads

2 tablespoons butter	1 cup water
½ cup celery, diced	½ teaspoon poultry seasoning
¼ cup onion, minced	1 cup long-grain rice
2 teaspoons orange rind, grated	⅓ cup golden raisins
1 cup orange juice	6 orange shells

Heat butter in medium-sized saucepan and sauté celery and onion until tender. Stir in orange rind, juice, water, poultry seasoning, rice, and raisins. Bring to a boil. Stir well, reduce heat, and cover. Simmer until liquid is absorbed and rice is tender, about 30 minutes.

Remove from heat. When cool, refrigerate for several hours. Serve in orange shells. Makes 6 servings.

Chicken Velvet Soup

1 chicken breast, cooked	1 tablespoon cornstarch
1 teaspoon salt	2 tablespoons cold water
2 egg whites, beaten until stiff peaks form	1 teaspoon sherry
3 cups chicken broth	2 tablespoons minced beef, cooked
1 small can cream-style corn	

Remove chicken meat from bones; mince. Mix with salt. Fold into egg whites.

Bring broth to boil. Add corn, cornstarch mixed with cold water, and sherry. Cook 2 minutes over low heat. Stir in chicken mixture. Bring to boil; remove from heat. Garnish each bowl with beef. Makes 6 servings.

Fruited Rice Salads

Egg Drop Soup

4 cups chicken broth, homemade or canned	Few sprinkles freshly ground pepper
1 tablespoon cornstarch	2 eggs, slightly beaten
¼ cup cold water	1 tablespoon fresh parsley, coarsely chopped
1 tablespoon soy sauce	
Pinch of grated fresh gingerroot, or a sprinkle of powdered ginger	A few cooked pea pods, or a small amount chopped scallions for garnish

Bring chicken broth to boil. Dissolve cornstarch in water, stir into broth, and bring to boil again. Add soy sauce, ginger, and pepper. Holding eggs above soup, slowly pour into soup in a slow, steady stream while whisking eggs into the soup to form long threads.

Turn off heat, add parsley, and garnish soup with pea pods or chopped scallions. If desired, warm chow mein noodles can be served with this soup. Makes 4 servings.

18/Soups and Salads

Hot-and-Sour Soup

¼ cup cloud ears	½ teaspoon hot oil
¼ cup golden needles	2 teaspoons sesame-seed oil
¼ pound pork, shredded into 1½-inch-long strips	4 cups chicken stock
	Salt to taste
3 tablespoons cornstarch	1 tablespoon soy sauce
2 teaspoons sherry	2 bean curds, each cut into 8 pieces
½ cup water	
3 tablespoons white-wine vinegar (or to taste)	1 egg, beaten
White pepper to taste	2 scallions, chopped

Soak cloud ears and golden needles in hot water about 15 minutes or until noticeably increased in size; drain. Shred cloud ears. Cut golden needles in half.

Combine pork with 1 tablespoon cornstarch and sherry. Mix 2 tablespoons cornstarch with water; set aside. Combine vinegar, pepper, hot oil, and sesame oil in bowl; set aside.

Bring chicken stock, salt, and soy sauce to boil in large soup pot. Add pork; boil 1 minute. Add cloud ears, golden needles, and bean curds; boil 1 minute. Add cornstarch mixture and stir until thickened. Lower heat. Add vinegar mixture. Taste; adjust seasoning if necessary. Slowly stir in egg. Garnish with scallions. Makes 5 or 6 servings.

Mandarin Soup

1 tablespoon oil	6 cups chicken broth, homemade or canned
½ pound pork, trimmed of fat and sliced into thin strips	¾ cup spinach, finely chopped
1 cup celery, chopped	MSG to taste (optional)
½ cup carrots, diced	1 egg, beaten
1 cup fresh mushrooms, sliced	2 tablespoons cornstarch
	¼ cup cold water

Heat oil in pot. Sauté pork 10 minutes. Add celery, carrots, and mushrooms; sauté 5 minutes. Stir in chicken broth, spinach, and MSG; bring to boil. Add egg, stirring constantly.

Mix cornstarch and water together. Add to soup and stir until soup is thickened. Makes 6 servings.

Black-Mushroom Soup

- ¼ cup dried black mushrooms
- 1 clove garlic, crushed
- 1 tablespoon sesame oil
- 8 cups rich chicken broth
- 1 piece of gingerroot, size of hazelnut
- 2½ tablespoons soy sauce
- ½ cup cooked chicken, finely diced
- ½ cup cooked ham, finely diced
- ½ cup bamboo shoots, diced
- ½ cup scallions, finely chopped

Soak mushrooms in warm water until soft and spongy, about 10 minutes. Squeeze out liquid and chop very fine. Crush garlic and sauté in oil for 2 or 3 seconds; remove from oil and set aside. Sauté the mushrooms in the same pan for about 5 minutes.

In soup kettle, bring chicken broth to boil. Add mushrooms, garlic, ginger, and soy sauce. Simmer about 4 hours. Strain the broth and add chicken, ham, bamboo shoots, and scallions. Simmer just until all ingredients are heated through. Makes 8 servings.

Celery Soup

20/Soups and Salads

Celery Soup

1	heaping tablespoon dried Chinese mushrooms	2	small onions, minced
2	small celeriac roots, with green tops (celery stalks can be substituted)	1	clove garlic, minced
		3	cups hot chicken broth, from cubes or homemade
4	tablespoons oil	2	quarts salted water
½	pound pork shoulder, cut into 1½-inch-long, ½-inch-thick strips	1	ounce Chinese transparent noodles
		2	tablespoons soy sauce
		⅛	teaspoon ground ginger

Soak mushrooms in cold water 30 minutes. Cut off celeriac tops; set aside. Brush celeriac roots under running cold water. Peel; cut into 1/2-inch cubes.

Heat oil in saucepan. Add pork; brown on all sides, stirring constantly, about 3 minutes. Add onions, garlic, and celeriac root; cook 5 minutes. Drain mushrooms; cut in halves, or quarters if very large. Add to saucepan. Pour in broth. Cover; simmer over low heat 25 minutes.

Meanwhile, bring salted water to boil in another saucepan. Add noodles. Remove from heat immediately; let stand 5 minutes. Drain noodles.

Five minutes before end of cooking time of soup, add coarsely chopped celeriac tops. Season to taste with soy sauce and ground ginger. Place noodles in soup tureen or 4 individual Chinese soup bowls. Pour soup over noodles. Serve immediately. Makes 4 servings.

Sharks'-Fin Soup

¾	pound dried sharks' fins	3	quarts chicken broth
1	tablespoon oil	2	tablespoons cornstarch
2	tablespoons fresh gingerroot, sliced	1	teaspoon soy sauce
		¼	cup water
¼	cup scallions, sliced	¼	teaspoon MSG (optional)
1	tablespoon sherry	½	pound crab meat

Wash sharks' fins; cover with cold water. Drain, then cover with fresh water. Boil 3 hours; drain. Add fresh water and boil 3 hours. Drain; let dry.

Heat oil in large saucepan. Sauté ginger and scallions 3 minutes. Add sherry, 1 quart chicken broth, and sharks' fins. Cook over medium-high heat 15 minutes. Drain any remaining liquid. Add remaining broth; bring to boil.

Mix together soy sauce, water, MSG, and cornstarch. Slowly stir into soup. Stir in crab meat; heat through. Makes about 8 servings.

Soup with Vegetables and Meat Dumplings

Crab Soup

- 2 tablespoons oil
- ½ pound crab meat
- ¼ teaspoon salt
- 2 medium tomatoes, coarsely chopped
- 1½ teaspoons fresh gingerroot, chopped
- 5 cups chicken broth
- 2 eggs, beaten
- 1½ tablespoons vinegar
- 1½ tablespoons sherry
- 1½ tablespoons soy sauce
- 3 scallions, sliced

Heat oil in large pot. Sauté crab meat, salt, tomatoes, and ginger 5 minutes. Add chicken broth; cook over low heat 10 minutes.

Beat eggs. Add vinegar, sherry, and soy sauce. Slowly pour into soup. Stir in scallions; let soup simmer about 3 minutes. Makes 4 to 6 servings.

22/Soups and Salads

Soup with Vegetables and Meat Dumplings

Meat Dumplings
2 slices bread
½ pound lean ground beef
Salt
White pepper
5 cups beef bouillon

Soup
¼ head savoy cabbage (green cabbage can be substituted), sliced
1 leek, sliced
2 ounces fresh mushrooms, sliced
1 celery stalk, sliced
1 tablespoon oil
1 small onion, chopped
2 ounces frozen peas
4 ounces egg noodles
Salt
White pepper
1 tablespoon soy sauce
3 tablespoons sherry

Soak bread in small amount of cold water. Squeeze as dry as possible and mix with ground beef and salt and pepper to taste. Bring bouillon to a boil. Using 1 teaspoon of meat mixture, form little dumplings and drop into boiling broth. Reduce heat and simmer for 10 minutes.

For soup, slice cabbage, leek, mushrooms, and celery. Heat oil in a large saucepan. Add onion and cook until golden. Add sliced vegetables and cook for 5 minutes. Remove dumplings from beef broth with a slotted spoon, drain on paper towels, and keep warm.

Strain broth and add to vegetables. Add peas and noodles and simmer for 15 minutes. Return dumplings to soup. Season with salt, pepper, soy sauce, and sherry. Serve immediately. Makes 4 to 6 servings.

Chicken Vegetable Soup

6 cups chicken broth
½ cup bean sprouts
¼ cup water chestnuts, thinly sliced
1 scallion, minced
½ cup bok choy, sliced (use leafy part also)
3 Chinese mushrooms, soaked and drained and sliced
½ cup snow pea pods
½ cup cooked chicken, diced
2 teaspoons soy sauce
1 tablespoon sherry
Pepper to taste

Bring chicken broth to boil in soup pot. Add vegetables and chicken and simmer about 1 minute. Add soy sauce and sherry. Add pepper to taste. If desired, cellophane noodles or very fine egg noodles may be added. Makes 4 to 6 servings.

Soups and Salads/21

Wonton Soup

24/Soups and Salads

Noodle Soup

2	tablespoons dried Chinese mushrooms	½	pound transparent noodles
½	pound boneless pork	5	ounces bamboo shoots
2	tablespoons sherry	2	quarts chicken broth
2	tablespoons soy sauce	3	tablespoons vegetable oil
Salt to taste		1	small can chicken meat, cut into 1-inch squares
White pepper to taste		5	ounces ham steak, cut into 1-inch squares
Pinch of ground ginger			
1	quart salted water	½	cup watercress, chopped

Soak mushrooms 30 minutes; drain well. Set aside.

Cut pork into 3-inch strips 1/8 inch thick. Combine sherry, soy sauce, salt, pepper, and ginger in bowl. Add pork. Let stand, covered, 1 hour.

Bring salted water to boil. Add noodles; cook 10 minutes. Drain well; set aside. Slice mushrooms and bamboo shoots. Add mushrooms, bamboo shoots, and noodles to chicken broth; simmer 2 minutes.

Remove pork from soy-sauce mixture; pat dry. Sauté pork in oil 2 minutes; remove. Add chicken, pork, and ham to broth. Add watercress. Spoon broth into individual soup bowls. Makes 6 servings.

Wonton Soup

Dumpling Dough

4 ounces flour
Salt
1 tablespoon milk
2 tablespoons oil
1 small egg

Filling
4 ounces fresh spinach, chopped

4 ounces ground pork
½ tablespoon soy sauce
⅛ teaspoon ground ginger

Soup
5 cups chicken broth
2 tablespoons chopped chives

Stir flour and salt together in bowl. Add milk, oil, and egg. Knead dough until smooth. Roll out dough on floured board until paper-thin. Cut into 3-inch squares. Cover with kitchen towel while preparing filling.

Thoroughly wash spinach and remove coarse stems. Place in bowl; barely cover with boiling water. Let stand 3 minutes, then drain well. Coarsely chop. Add pork, soy sauce, and ginger; blend thoroughly. Place 1 teaspoon filling on each dough square, giving filling lengthy shape. Fold over dough from one side; roll up jelly-roll fashion. Press ends of roll together to seal.

Bring broth to boil. Add wontons, simmer over low heat 20 minutes. Spoon into bowls. Garnish with chives. Makes 6 servings.

Soups and Salads/25

Chicken Chow Mein

Poultry Main Courses

Chicken Cantonese

½ **pound white meat of chicken, sliced in strips about 1½ inches long and ½-inch wide**
½ **pound snow peas, strings removed**
¼ **cup peanut oil**
¼ **cup bamboo shoots**
1 **cup bok choy, sliced**
1 **cup fresh mushrooms, sliced**
1 **cup celery, sliced diagonally**
¼ **cup water chestnuts, sliced**
1 **teaspoon MSG (optional)**
4 **cups chicken stock**
2 **tablespoons cornstarch mixed with ½ cup cold water**

Slice chicken and set aside. Wash snow peas, remove strings, and set aside. Heat oil in skillet or wok and stir-fry chicken for about 10 seconds. Add bamboo shoots, bok choy, mushrooms, celery, water chestnuts, and MSG; stir-fry for another 10 seconds. Add chicken stock, bring to a boil, cover, and simmer for about 1 minute. Stir in cornstarch mixture and mix thoroughly. Serve immediately. Makes 3 to 4 servings.

Sweet-and-Sour Barbecued Chicken

28/Poultry Main Courses

Barbecued Chicken

¼ cup soy sauce	1 teaspoon sugar
2 cloves garlic, minced	2 tablespoons oil
2 teaspoons salt	1 roasting chicken,
¼ teaspoon black pepper, freshly ground	approximately 4 pounds, whole, washed and dried
1 teaspoon five-spice	

Mix soy sauce, garlic, salt, pepper, five-spice, sugar, and oil together. Rub into inside and outside of chicken. Let stand 1 hour. Place chicken on rack in shallow roasting pan. Roast in 425°F oven 2-1/2 hours or until chicken is tender and nicely browned. Turn and baste often.

To serve, chicken can be cut up with bones left on (American-style), or meat can be taken off bones and cut into pieces about 1 inch square (Chinese-style). Makes about 4 servings.

Chicken Chow Mein

1 green sweet pepper, cut into slices	1 (4-ounce) can sliced mushrooms, drained
1 red sweet pepper, cut into slices	8 ounces cooked chicken breast, cut into bite-sized pieces
1 cup boiling water	6 cups water
1½ tablespoons butter	8 ounces egg noodles
1 small onion, chopped	Salt
2 stalks celery, sliced	1 tablespoon butter
1 tablespoon flour	Oil for frying
1 cup chicken broth	4 ounces sliced almonds,
2 tablespoons soy sauce	toasted and slightly salted
Freshly ground pepper to taste	

Cut green and red peppers into slices. Blanch in boiling water for 5 minutes. Remove and drain. Heat 1-1/2 tablespoons butter in saucepan. Add onions and celery and sauté until onions are transparent. Sprinkle with flour, pour in chicken broth, and bring to a boil while stirring constantly. Simmer for 10 minutes. Season with soy sauce and pepper. Add pepper slices, drained mushrooms, and chicken pieces. Cover and simmer for 15 minutes.

Meanwhile, bring 6 cups of slightly salted water to a boil; add noodles and cook for 15 minutes. Drain and rinse with cold water. Set aside 1/3 of the noodles. Place rest of noodles in heated bowl. Add 1 tablespoon butter, cover, and keep warm.

Heat oil in skillet until very hot. Cut noodles that were set aside into approximately 2-inch-long pieces. Add to hot oil and fry until golden. Drain on paper towels. To serve, spoon chicken mixture over buttered noodles; top with fried noodles and toasted almonds. Makes 4 servings.

Poultry Main Courses/29

Chinese Fish

30/Poultry Main Courses

Chicken with Dates

1   **chicken, approximately 3 to 3½ pounds**
Salt
Pepper
Curry powder
2   **tablespoons oil**
1   **medium-sized onion, chopped**
2   **green peppers, cut into thin strips**

1   **cup beef bouillon**
½   **pound rice**
1   **teaspoon cornstarch**
12   **dates, pitted and cut into halves**
1   **cup yogurt**
3   **tablespoons sliced almonds, toasted**

Divide chicken into 8 pieces. Remove all except wing and leg bones. Rub chicken with salt, pepper, and curry powder. Heat oil in heavy skillet. Add chicken; cook until golden on all sides. Add onion; cook until golden. Add green peppers. Pour in bouillon; simmer over low heat 30 minutes.

Meanwhile, cook rice according to package directions.

Remove chicken from sauce; keep warm. Strain sauce. Blend cornstarch with small amount cold water. Slowly stir into sauce; cook until thick and bubbly. Add dates. Beat yogurt with fork; stir into sauce. If necessary, correct seasonings. Heat through, but do not boil.

Spoon rice into bowl or platter; arrange chicken on top. Pour sauce over chicken; top with almonds. Makes 4 or 5 servings.

Cashew Chicken

2   **tablespoons oil**
½   **teaspoon salt**
1   **cup chicken breast meat, sliced**
¾   **cup pea pods**
½   **cup bamboo shoots**
½   **cup fresh mushrooms, sliced**

1   **cup chicken broth**
½   **cup cashew nuts (or as desired)**
¼   **teaspoon sugar**
¼   **teaspoon MSG (optional)**
½   **teaspoon cornstarch**
1   **teaspoon water**

Coat preheated wok with oil (swirl around). Sprinkle in salt. Stir-fry chicken 2 minutes. Add pea pods, bamboo shoots, mushrooms, and chicken broth. Cover wok and cook 2 minutes. Carefully stir in nuts, sugar, and MSG.

Mix cornstarch with water; stir into chicken mixture until thickened. Makes 4 servings.

Fish in Sweet-and-Sour Sauce

Lemon Chicken

1	(3-pound) chicken	½	teaspoon powdered ginger
1½	teaspoons salt, divided	1	cup chicken broth
2	tablespoons soy sauce	¼	cup lemon juice
2	tablespoons brandy	½	teaspoon sugar
5	tablespoons safflower oil		

Rub inside of chicken with 1 teaspoon of the salt. Rub outside with soy sauce. Place in deep bowl and pour brandy over the chicken. Marinate for 6 hours, turning chicken frequently. Drain and reserve marinade.

In a wok, over medium-high heat, combine oil and ginger. Brown chicken on all sides. Reduce heat to low and add marinade, chicken broth, lemon juice, sugar, and remaining 1/2 teaspoon salt. Cover wok and simmer for about 25 minutes, or until chicken is tender. Place on serving platter, cut into pieces, and pour juices in wok over the chicken. Makes 4 servings.

Curried Shrimp

Chicken Balls in Oyster Sauce

- 2 raw chicken breasts, skin and bones discarded
- 2 scallions
- 1 teaspoon salt
- 1 tablespoon cornstarch
- 1 tablespoon sherry
- 2 tablespoons water
- Oil for frying
- ½ cup onions, thinly sliced
- 1 teaspoon sugar
- ½ teaspoon fresh gingerroot, chopped
- 2 tablespoons oyster sauce
- ¼ cup chicken broth
- Freshly ground black pepper to taste

Chop chicken and scallions together until very fine. Mix in salt, cornstarch, sherry, and water. Shape into small balls.

Heat oil in skillet, fry the balls until browned on all sides. Pour off the oil. Add onions, sugar, ginger, oyster sauce, and chicken broth. Cook and stir over low heat 5 minutes. Sprinkle with pepper. Makes 4 servings.

Poultry Main Courses/33

Kang Pao Chicken

12 ounces boned chicken, cut into ½-inch squares	1 tablespoon white rice-wine vinegar
1 egg white	2 tablespoons water
2 teaspoons cornstarch	2 teaspoons garlic, minced
2 tablespoons brown bean sauce	1 cup peanut oil
1 tablespoon hoisin sauce	1¼ teaspoons crushed red pepper (or as desired)
2 teaspoons sherry	½ cup roasted peanuts
1 teaspoon sugar	

Combine chicken with egg white and cornstarch in bowl. Mash bean sauce in separate bowl. Add hoisin sauce, sherry, sugar, vinegar, water, and garlic.

Heat wok over high heat. Add oil. When oil is very hot, add chicken; stir 30 seconds or until chicken changes color. Remove from wok; set aside.

Drain off all but 2 tablespoons oil. Reheat wok. When oil is very hot, add red pepper; stir 25 seconds or until pepper darkens. Add chicken, bean-sauce mixture, and peanuts to wok; stir 1 minute or until heated through. Makes 2 or 3 servings.

Oriental Chicken

4 ounces almonds, slivered	1 cucumber, unpeeled and thinly sliced
3 tablespoons peanut oil	½ cup chicken stock
¾ cup onion, chopped	2 teaspoons sherry
4 chicken breasts, boned and thinly sliced	¼ teaspoon ground ginger
2 cans (approximately 6 ounces each) sliced bamboo shoots, drained	1 teaspoon soy sauce
	½ teaspoon cornstarch
	1 tablespoon cold water
1 can water chestnuts, drained and sliced	Salt to taste
	Freshly ground pepper to taste

Brown almonds in 400°F oven about 10 minutes. Watch closely. Set aside.

Pour oil into large frying pan or wok; heat to medium-high heat. Add onion; cook until limp. Remove onion from pan (push up side, if using wok). Add chicken to pan; toss gently about 1 minute. Add bamboo shoots and water chestnuts; toss gently 1 minute. Add cucumber; cook 1 minute.

Combine stock, sherry, ginger, and soy sauce. Add to pan; cook 1 minute. Combine cornstarch and water in small dish. Stir slowly into hot mixture. Season with salt and pepper. Cook until liquid is thickened.

While cooking, return onions to mixture. Serve chicken with rice and browned almonds. Makes 4 servings.

34/Poultry Main Courses

Roast Chicken

4 scallions, chopped
2 small pieces fresh
   gingerroot
1 cup soy sauce
½ cup sherry
1 teaspoon sugar

¼ teaspoon salt
4 cups water
1 whole chicken, about 3
   pounds
Scallions for garnish

Mix chopped scallions, gingerroot, soy sauce, sherry, sugar, and salt together. Add water to stew pot. Mix in scallion mixture. Bring to a boil. Wash chicken, place in pot, cover, and simmer for 30 minutes.

Remove chicken from pot and place on roasting rack in pan. Roast in 350°F oven for 45 minutes, or until chicken is tender and browned. Split chicken in half, and cut each half into 5 to 6 pieces. Arrange, skin-side-up, on serving platter. Garnish with scallions. Serve the broth as a dipping sauce. Makes 4 servings.

Sesame Chicken

1 (2- to 2½-pound) chicken,
   washed, dried, and
   disjointed
Flour, seasoned with salt and
   freshly ground black
   pepper
2 eggs, beaten
2 tablespoons milk
1 cup flour
½ cup sesame seeds
½ teaspoon salt
¼ teaspoon freshly ground
   black pepper
Peanut oil for frying

Light Cream Sauce
4 tablespoons butter
4 tablespoons flour
½ cup half-and-half
1 cup chicken stock
½ cup whipping cream
Onion salt to taste
Freshly ground black pepper
   to taste

Dust chicken with seasoned flour. Mix together eggs and milk. Dip floured chicken into milk mixture. Mix 1 cup flour with sesame seeds, salt, and pepper. Roll chicken in mixture. Deep-fry in oil until light brown and tender. Serve with Light Cream Sauce.

To make sauce, melt butter over low heat. Add flour; blend, stirring constantly, several minutes. Mix half-and-half, stock, and whipping cream together. Gradually add to butter and flour, stirring constantly. When mixture is smooth, stir in onion salt and pepper. Let cook over hot water in double boiler about 15 minutes, stirring occasionally.

Serve the sauce with the Sesame Chicken. Makes 4 servings.

Ginger Beef

Poultry Main Courses/35

36/Poultry Main Courses

Chicken with Sweet Peppers

2 **whole chicken breasts, boned and cut into 1-inch pieces**
2 **cloves garlic, pressed**
4 **tablespoons olive oil**
3 **tablespoons soy sauce**
½ **teaspoon salt**
¼ **teaspoon freshly ground black pepper**
2 **teaspoons cornstarch**
2 **green peppers, seeds and membrane removed, cut into 1-inch pieces**
1 **red pepper, seeds and membrane removed, cut into 1-inch pieces**
8 **green onions, cut into ½-inch pieces**
3 **celery stalks, cut into ½-inch pieces**
¼ **teaspoon sugar**
¼ **cup cold water**

Combine chicken, garlic, 1 tablespoon oil, 2 tablespoons soy sauce, salt, pepper, and 1 teaspoon cornstarch in mixing bowl; mix well. Let marinate at least 30 minutes.

Heat 3 tablespoons oil in wok. Add peppers; stir-fry 3 minutes. Add onions and celery; stir-fry 2 minutes. Using slotted spoon, remove vegetables; keep warm.

Place chicken in hot oil in wok; stir-fry 5 minutes. Combine 1 tablespoon soy sauce, 1 teaspoon cornstarch, sugar, and water. Pour over chicken. Carefully mix in vegetables and cook over low heat about 2 minutes or until heated through. Makes about 4 servings.

Chicken with Walnuts

1 **pound white chicken meat, cut into 1-inch cubes**
1 **teaspoon salt**
1 **teaspoon sugar**
1 **tablespoon soy sauce**
3 **tablespoons sherry**
2 **tablespoons cornstarch**
1 **egg, beaten**
½ **cup peanut oil**
1 **cup walnuts**
2 **teaspoons fresh gingerroot, minced**
3 **cloves garlic, minced**
½ **cup boiling water**
MSG to taste (optional)
1 **cup bamboo shoots, sliced**

Combine chicken in bowl with salt, sugar, soy sauce, and sherry; mix well. Let stand 30 minutes. Drain; reserve marinade. Dip chicken pieces into cornstarch, then into egg.

Heat oil in wok or deep skillet; brown walnuts. Remove walnuts; pour off all but 2 tablespoons oil. Brown chicken, ginger, and garlic. Add water, MSG, bamboo shoots, and marinade. Cover; cook over low heat 10 minutes. Add walnuts and mix through. Makes 4 servings.

Poultry Main Courses/37

Deep-Fried Sweet-and-Sour Chicken

2	tablespoons cornstarch	*Sweet-and-Sour Sauce*	
2	tablespoons soy sauce	¾	cup sugar
1	teaspoon salt	2	tablespoons soy sauce
2	eggs	1	tablespoon dry white wine
Oil for cooking		3	tablespoons wine vinegar
1	(4-pound) cooked chicken,	3	tablespoons catsup
	boned, skinned, and meat	2	tablespoons cornstarch
	cut into 1-inch cubes	½	cup water

Combine cornstarch and soy sauce; mix well. Combine salt and eggs in mixing bowl; beat with whisk until light. Stir in cornstarch mixture until just mixed.

Heat oil in deep-fryer to 375°F, or until small ball of flour mixed with water dropped into oil floats to top immediately. Dip chicken into egg mixture; drain slightly. Drop chicken, several cubes at a time, into oil. Fry until lightly browned; drain on paper towels. Place chicken in individual serving dishes.

To make sauce, combine sugar, soy sauce, wine, vinegar, and catsup in saucepan; bring to boil. Dissolve cornstarch in water; add to sauce. Cook over low heat, stirring, until sauce has thickened. Spoon sauce over the chicken. Makes 4 to 6 servings.

Chicken with Vegetables

¼	cup soy sauce	1	medium-sized zucchini, thinly sliced
¼	cup chicken broth		
2	whole chicken breasts, skinned, boned, and cut into bite-sized pieces	6	ounces snow-pea pods, fresh or frozen
4	tablespoons peanut oil	½	pound fresh mushrooms, sliced
1	clove garlic, minced	Boiled rice	
2	small yellow squash, thinly sliced		

Mix soy sauce with broth in shallow bowl. Marinate chicken in mixture at least 1 hour. Heat 2 tablespoons oil in wok until sizzling. Add garlic; cook 2 minutes. Drain chicken; reserve marinade. Cook chicken in wok, stirring constantly, 2 minutes. Remove from wok; keep warm.

Add 2 tablespoons oil to wok; heat. Add squash and zucchini; stir-fry until coated with oil. Push to one side. Add pea pods and mushrooms; toss to coat with oil. Add chicken and soy-sauce mixture; cover. Reduce heat and simmer 5 minutes or until vegetables are tender but still crispy. Serve with rice. Makes 4 servings.

38/Poultry Main Courses

Chicken with Pineapple

1	chicken, approximately 2½ to 3 pounds, boned	2	tablespoons oil
		1	cup pineapple chunks, drained, reserving pineapple juice

Marinade

2	tablespoons cornstarch
3	tablespoons oil
4	tablespoons soy sauce
1	tablespoon sherry
Salt	
Pepper	

Gravy

1	tablespoon oil
1	clove garlic, minced
½	cup pineapple juice
2	tablespoons sherry

Bone chicken and cut meat into bite-sized pieces. Combine ingredients for marinade and blend thoroughly. Pour over chicken pieces, cover, and refrigerate for 30 minutes.

Heat 2 tablespoons oil in heavy skillet. Drain chicken, reserving marinade. Add chicken to skillet and brown for about 5 minutes while stirring constantly. Add drained pineapple chunks. Cover skillet and simmer over low heat for 12 minutes. Remove chicken and pineapple chunks with slotted spoon. Arrange on preheated platter and keep warm.

Add additional 1 tablespoon oil to pan drippings. Stir in minced garlic and cook for 5 minutes. Blend pineapple juice with reserved marinade and sherry. Pour into skillet and heat through. Strain sauce through sieve, spoon over chicken and pineapple, and serve immediately. Makes 4 servings.

Chicken Velvet

Meat from 2 chicken breasts, minced	
2	teaspoons cornstarch
¼	cup cold water
Pinch of salt	
3	egg whites, beaten until stiff peaks form
Vegetable oil for frying	
2	ounces snow-pea pods, cut in half
1	tablespoon oil

Sauce

1	teaspoon cornstarch
1	teaspoon cold water
½	cup chicken broth
1	tablespoon sherry
1	tablespoon vegetable oil

Mix chicken with cornstarch, water, and salt. Fold mixture into egg whites. Drop by teaspoonfuls into hot oil; cook until lightly browned. Drain on paper towels.

Sauté pea pods in 1 tablespoon oil until well coated.

Mix cornstarch with cold water in small saucepan until smooth. Add rest of ingredients; bring to boil. Add sauce and chicken to snow peas. Bring to boil. Makes 2 servings.

Sweet-and-Sour Barbecued Chicken

- 1 (2½-pound) chicken
- 4 tablespoons margarine
- 2 level tablespoons brown sugar
- 4 tablespoons lemon juice
- 1 tablespoon soy sauce
- ¼ level teaspoon ground cinnamon
- Salt and pepper

Divide chicken into 4 portions. Put remaining ingredients in a saucepan and heat, stirring, until smooth. Brush sweet-and-sour mixture over chicken portions. Cook chicken on a grill or in the broiler until tender, basting frequently and turning occasionally, for 30 to 40 minutes. Makes 4 servings.

Beef Slices Peking

40/Poultry Main Courses

Chicken with Mandarin Oranges and Almonds

2 ounces seedless raisins	1 clove garlic, minced
1 jigger Madeira	½ cup hot beef bouillon
1 large chicken, 3½ to 4 pounds, cut into serving pieces	1 tablespoon cornstarch
	1 tablespoon soy sauce
2 teaspoons paprika	½ teaspoon powdered ginger
1 teaspoon white pepper	½ cup heavy cream, lightly beaten
5 tablespoons oil	1 tablespoon butter
1 (11-ounce) can mandarin oranges, drained	2 tablespoons sliced almonds

Cover raisins with Madeira and soak. Cut chicken into serving pieces. Mix paprika and pepper together, and rub chicken with this mixture.

Heat oil in skillet or Dutch oven. Add chicken and fry until golden on all sides, about 10 minutes. Drain mandarin oranges, reserving juice. Measure 1/2 cup of juice and pour over chicken. Add minced garlic. Pour in beef bouillon, cover, and simmer for 30 minutes. Drain raisins and add; cook for another 5 minutes.

Remove chicken with slotted spoon. Arrange on preheated platter and keep warm. Blend cornstarch with small amount of cold water; add to sauce, stirring constantly until thickened and bubbly. Season with soy sauce and powdered ginger. Add mandarin oranges and lightly beaten heavy cream. Heat through, but do not boil.

Heat butter in small skillet. Add sliced almonds and cook until golden. Pour sauce over chicken and top with almonds. Makes 6 servings.

Paper-Wrapped Chicken

1 pound chicken meat, very thinly sliced	1 teaspoon fresh gingerroot, grated
2 tablespoons soy sauce	16 pieces cooking parchment; if unavailable, use foil, approximately 4 inches square
1 tablespoon dry sherry	
½ teaspoon brown sugar	
½ teaspoon salt	
1 scallion, thinly sliced	Vegetable oil for frying

Combine chicken, soy sauce, sherry, brown sugar, salt, scallion, and ginger. Marinate 30 minutes. Divide chicken mixture into 16 portions. Wrap each portion in piece of cooking parchment; fasten well.

Heat oil in wok to 375°F. Deep-fry packages a few at a time 3 minutes. Drain on paper towels; keep hot. Serve wrapped to keep in juices. Each is unwrapped just before eating. Makes 4 servings.

Poultry Main Courses/41

Pineapple Duck

1	duck, about 4 pounds
4	slices canned pineapple
1	large green pepper, cut into 1-inch squares
2	tablespoons oil
1	teaspoon salt
¼	teaspoon pepper
½	teaspoon MSG (optional)
1	tablespoon soy sauce
1	tablespoon cornstarch mixed with 2 tablespoons cold water

Clean and quarter duck. Cover with boiling water and simmer gently until tender. Remove from broth and let duck drain. Reserve broth. Cut each slice of pineapple into 8 pieces. Cut pepper into squares.

Preheat skillet and add oil. Place pieces of duck in skillet, along with salt and pepper. Brown gently, turning frequently. When browned, add the pineapple and green pepper and stir-fry a few seconds. Add the broth, MSG, and soy sauce. Cover and simmer about 10 minutes. Thicken slightly with cornstarch mixture. Serve with rice. Makes 3 servings.

Stir-Fried Beef and Mushrooms

Meat Platter Szechwan

Peking Duck

1	(4- to 5-pound) duck	*Sauce*	
6	cups water	¼	cup hoisin sauce
¼	cup honey	1	tablespoon water
4	slices of fresh gingerroot, about 1 inch in diameter and ⅛ inch thick	1	teaspoon sesame-seed oil
		2	teaspoons sugar
		12	scallion brushes
2	scallions, sliced	**Mandarin Pancakes (see next recipe)**	

Wash duck thoroughly with cold water, and dry. Tie a cord tightly around neck skin and suspend duck in an airy place to dry the skin (about 3 hours).

Bring water to boil. Add honey, gingerroot, and sliced scallions. Lower duck by its string into the boiling liquid and moisten the duck's skin

Poultry Main Courses/43

thoroughly, using a spoon. Suspend duck by its cord until it is dry (about 3 hours).

Make sauce by combining all sauce ingredients in a small pan; stir until sugar dissolves. Bring to a boil, then simmer for 3 minutes. Set aside to cool.

Cut scallions to 3-inch lengths and trim off roots. Stand each scallion on end and make 4 intersecting cuts 1 inch deep into its stalk. Repeat at other end. Place scallions in ice water and refrigerate until cut parts curl. Preheat oven to 375°F.

Untie duck and cut off any loose neck skin. Place duck, breast-side-up, on a rack and set in a roasting pan. Roast for 1 hour. Lower heat to 300°F, turn duck on its breast, and roast for 30 minutes longer. Raise heat to 375°F, return duck to its back, and roast for 30 minutes. Transfer to carving board.

With small, sharp knife and using your fingers, remove crisp skin from breast, sides, and back of duck. Cut skin into 2- by 3-inch rectangles and arrange them in a single layer on a platter. Cut wings and drumsticks from duck, and cut all meat away from breast and carcass. Slice meat into pieces 2-1/2 inches long and 1/2 inch wide, and arrange them on another platter.

Serve duck with Mandarin pancakes, sauce, and the scallion brushes. Dip a scallion brush into the sauce and brush a pancake with it. The scallion is placed in the middle of the pancake with a piece of duck skin and a piece of meat. The pancake is rolled around the pieces and eaten like a sandwich. Makes approximately 6 servings.

Mandarin Pancakes

2   cups all-purpose flour, sifted
¾ cup boiling water

1 to 2 tablespoons sesame-seed oil

Put sifted flour in bowl; make a well in flour and pour water into it. Mix with wooden spoon until soft dough. Knead dough gently on lightly floured surface 10 minutes. It should be smooth. Let rest under damp kitchen towel 15 minutes.

On lightly floured surface roll dough to about 1/4 inch thick. With 2-1/2-inch glass, cut as many circles as you can. Use scraps of dough, kneading them again and cutting out more circles. Brush half of circles lightly with sesame-seed oil. Place unoiled circle on top of oiled one. Flatten each pair with rolling pin to diameter of 6 inches. Turn once to roll both sides, trying to keep circular shape. Cover pancakes with dry towel.

Heat 8-inch, ungreased skillet to high heat. Reduce heat to moderate. Cook pancakes 1 at a time, turning them as little bubbles and brown specks appear. Cook about 1 minute on each side. As each pancake is cooked, gently separate halves; stack on plate. Makes about 24.

Chinese Duck

2 cups sherry
½ cup honey
2 tablespoons soy sauce
2 tablespoons candied ginger, finely chopped
2 teaspoons powdered mustard
1 teaspoon sesame seeds
1 (3- to 4-pound) duck
Salt
2 tablespoons margarine

2 to 3 tablespoons sugar
¼ cup sherry
1 teaspoon cornstarch
1 (11-ounce) can mandarin orange sections
1 banana

Garnish
1 orange, sliced
2 maraschino cherries
Parsley sprigs

Orange Sauce
6 oranges
1 piece of candied ginger, approximately size of a walnut, chopped

Blend thoroughly sherry, honey, soy sauce, finely chopped ginger, mustard, and sesame seeds. Pour over duck in large bowl, cover, and refrigerate for 3 hours, turning duck occasionally. Remove duck and drain well on paper towels. Reserve marinade. Salt inside of duck lightly.

Heat margarine in large skillet or Dutch oven. Add duck and brown well on all sides. Place duck in preheated 350°F oven and cook for 1 hour and 10 minutes, basting occasionally with reserved marinade.

To prepare sauce, pare half an orange and cut rind into thin strips. Now squeeze oranges. Blend orange juice, sliced rind, and chopped ginger. Add sugar and half the sherry. Heat mixture in saucepan. Blend rest of sherry with cornstarch, and slowly add to orange sauce, stirring constantly until thick and bubbly. Drain mandarin orange sections and slice banana. Add half of the fruit to sauce.

Place duck on preheated platter. Garnish with rest of mandarins, banana and orange slices, cherries, and parsley. Serve sauce separately. Makes about 4 servings.

Marinated Steak Slices

Crispy Duck

1	duck, about 4 pounds
6	small slices fresh gingerroot
3	tablespoons salt
4	scallions, finely chopped
1	teaspoon Szechwan peppercorns
1	tablespoon rice wine or sherry
4	star anise
3	tablespoons soy sauce
	Oil for deep frying

Coat duck well with mixture of gingerroot, salt, scallions, peppercorns, rice wine, and star anise. Let stand 30 minutes. Steam duck about 1 hour or until very tender. Remove; rub with soy sauce.

Deep-fry until golden brown. Cut meat into bite-sized pieces. Arrange on serving platter. Makes about 3 servings.

46/Poultry Main Courses

Szechwan Duck

4	slices fresh gingerroot, minced		***Lotus-Leaf Rolls***
4	scallions, finely chopped	1	cup flour
2	tablespoons salt	2	teaspoons sugar
1	tablespoon Szechwan peppercorns	2	teaspoons baking powder
1	(4- to 5-pound) duck, washed and cleaned	½	cup milk (water can be substituted)
1	quart vegetable oil		Oil
2	tablespoons salt mixed with 1 teaspoon peppercorns, roasted in oven 10 minutes		

Mix gingerroot, scallions, salt, and peppercorns together. Rub inside and outside of duck with mixture. Press on breastbone of duck; break to flatten it. Refrigerate overnight. Steam duck 2 hours; cool thoroughly.

Heat oil in wok or deep pot to 375°F. Deep-fry duck about 7 minutes or until golden brown and crisp.

Diner takes meat off bones (comes off easily with chopsticks), dips it into roasted salt-and-peppercorn mixture, then makes sandwich on a lotus-leaf roll.

To make lotus-leaf rolls: Mix flour with sugar and baking powder. Slowly add milk; stir with fork until dough is soft. Knead 5 minutes. Cover with clean, dry cloth; let stand 15 minutes. Knead 2 minutes. Make about 1-inch diameter roll from dough. Cut into pieces about 1 inch thick. Brush with small amount oil; fold over. Use fork to make indentations all around edge. Steam 8 minutes over medium-high heat. Makes 4 servings.

Mandarin Liver

Fish and Seafood
Main Courses

Halibut Cantonese

1½ pounds halibut, cut into small chunks
1 tablespoon oil
1 medium-sized onion, chopped

Sauce
1½ cups water
1 tablespoon oil
Pinch salt
3 teaspoons soy sauce
1 teaspoon MSG (optional)

Pinch of freshly ground pepper
2 tablespoons cornstarch dissolved in 3 tablespoons water

2 cloves garlic, minced
1 scallion, sliced
1 tablespoon celery, chopped
1 egg, beaten

Boil halibut in a pot of water for 2 minutes. Heat oil in a skillet and brown onion. Transfer fish to skillet. Mix together the sauce ingredients, except for the cornstarch and water. Pour the sauce on the fish, and add garlic, scallion, and celery. Cover skillet and simmer for 2 minutes.

Pour beaten egg slowly into sauce, mixing constantly. Mix cornstarch with water and stir into sauce. Cook until thickened. Makes 2 servings.

Chop Suey

50/Fish and Seafood Main Courses

Poached Fish Mandarin-Style

½ **teaspoon fresh gingerroot, shredded**
2 **scallions, cut into 1-inch pieces**
1 **tablespoon soy sauce**
1 **tablespoon peanut oil**
1 **tablespoon sherry**

1 **whole fresh fish, about 1½ to 2 pounds (bass, flounder, sole, butterfish, whitefish), cleaned, washed, dried inside and out**

Mix ginger, scallions, soy sauce, oil, and sherry together. Rub mixture all over fish, inside and out.

Place water in bottom of wok; put fish on rack in wok, making sure water does not touch fish. Steam over high heat about 20 minutes or until fish is done. Makes 3 or 4 servings.

Chinese Fish

1 **whole trout, about 1 pound**
1 **whole carp, about 3 pounds**
Juice of 1 lemon
Salt
White pepper
2 **slices lean bacon**
Margarine to grease pan
4 **large leaves savoy cabbage (if unavailable, use regular cabbage)**
1 **pound fresh mushrooms**

2 **pieces sugared ginger**
3 **tablespoons soy sauce**
Pinch of ground anise
1 **cup hot water**
2 **teaspoons cornstarch**
2 **tablespoons bacon drippings**
Juice of half a lemon

Garnish
2 **tablespoons parsley, chopped**
Lemon slices

Have fishmonger scale and clean out the insides of the fish, but leave whole. At home wash fish thoroughly under running water; pat dry and rub with lemon juice. With sharp knife, make shallow incisions in backs of both fish and rub with salt and pepper. Cut bacon into small strips and insert one strip in each incision. Grease ovenproof baking dish with margarine and line with cabbage leaves. Place fish on top. Slice mushrooms and sugared ginger. Mix together and spoon over fish.

Sprinkle with soy sauce and ground anise. Pour in small amount of hot water. Cover with lid or aluminum foil and place in preheated oven at 350°F. Bake for 30 minutes. While baking, gradually add rest of hot water and baste fish with pan drippings.

Remove fish and cabbage leaves from pan. Arrange on a preheated platter. Bring pan drippings to a boil, scraping all brown particles from bottom of pan and adding some more water, if necessary.

Fish and Seafood Main Courses/51

Blend cornstarch with small amount of cold water, add to pan drippings, and stir until sauce is smooth and bubbly. Correct seasoning if necessary, and serve separately. Melt and heat bacon drippings. Pour over fish and sprinkle with lemon juice. Garnish fish with chopped parsley and lemon slices. Makes about 4 servings.

Sesame Salmon

3 salmon steaks, cut into thirds	1 tablespoon sesame seeds
1 green pepper, cut into thin strips	2 teaspoons vinegar
	1 tablespoon sesame-seed oil
1 leek, cut into thin strips	2 tablespoons soy sauce
2 cloves garlic, minced	2 teaspoons sugar
½ red chili pepper, minced	3 tablespoons water

Combine all ingredients except Fish. Pour marinade over salmon steaks; let stand 45 minutes. Preheat oven to 400°F. Wrap each piece of fish in foil; bake until tender, about 20 to 25 minutes. Makes 3 servings.

Vegetables with Pork

52/Fish and Seafood Main Courses

Fish in Sweet-and-Sour Sauce

1 **pound white fish fillets, skinned**
2 **carrots, sliced lengthwise**
3 **sticks celery, cut diagonally**
3 **tablespoons oil**
4 **tablespoons vinegar**
4 **level tablespoons sugar**

1 **level teaspoon fresh ginger, finely chopped**
½ **level teaspoon salt**
½ **level tablespoon cornstarch**
3 **tomatoes, skinned and coarsely chopped**

Cut fish into 1-inch pieces. Place carrots and celery in boiling salted water for 5 minutes, then drain. Heat oil in a wok, add fish pieces, and fry gently for 5 to 7 minutes or until cooked. Remove fish and drain.

Pour off excess oil from wok. Stir in vinegar, sugar, ginger, salt, cornstarch, tomatoes, carrots, celery, and 1/2 cup water. Bring to a boil, stirring continuously; add fish and reheat. Serve in a warm dish. Makes 4 to 6 servings.

Steamed Whole Fish

1½ **pounds whole fish (flounder, pike, trout, or sea bass)**
1 **teaspoon salt**
½ **teaspoon freshly ground pepper**
¼ **teaspoon powdered ginger**
3 **cups water**
2 **teaspoons mixed pickling spices (or more if you prefer it spicier)**

2 **bay leaves**
2 **cloves garlic, cut in half**
2 **tablespoons scallion, chopped**

Garnish
Lemon slices
Tomato
Parsley

Have fish scaled and cleaned and head removed, if you prefer. Lightly score the skin so seasonings will flavor fish. Combine salt, pepper, and ginger and rub on fish thoroughly. Pour water into large frying pan or wok and add pickling spices, bay leaves, garlic, and scallion. Place rack in pan or wok so that the fish will sit above the liquid, in order to allow the steam to circulate.

Place fish on the rack, cover, and let simmer for approximately 30 minutes, or until fish is tender. Garnish with lemon slices, tomato, and parsley. Makes 3 servings.

Slow Roast Spareribs

54/Fish and Seafood Main Courses

Oysters in Ginger Sauce

1	pint oysters, preferably small ones	3	tablespoons sherry
⅛	teaspoon five-spice powder	10	whole scallions
1½	teaspoons cornstarch	2	tablespoons oil
4	teaspoons soy sauce	4	thin slices fresh gingerroot

Mix oysters with five-spice powder, 1 teaspoon cornstarch, and 1 teaspoon soy sauce; set aside. Blend 1/2 teaspoon cornstarch, 3 teaspoons soy sauce, and sherry; set aside. Cut white part from scallions; cut each in half crosswise. Cut green parts into 1-inch sections.

Heat oil in wok or large frying pan over high heat. Add ginger and white parts of onions; cook and stir about 1 minute. Remove onion from pan; set aside. Spread out oysters in pan. Lower heat to medium; cook until oysters are just firm, turning once. Remove oysters from pan.

Cook drippings until browned. Blend in cornstarch-sherry mixture; cook and stir until thickened. Blend in whites and greens of onions and oysters; heat through until mixture simmers. Makes 2 servings.

Curried Shrimp

1	pound fresh shrimp, shelled and cleaned	1	medium-sized onion, chopped
	Juice of 1 lemon	½	teaspoon ground ginger
1	egg white	1	green pepper, thinly sliced
1	tablespoon cornstarch	2	teaspoons curry powder
2	cups sesame-seed or vegetable oil	1	teaspoon sugar
1	tablespoon dried Chinese mushrooms	2	tablespoons soy sauce
1	can (approximately 6 ounces) bamboo shoots	1	(8-ounce) can tiny peas, drained
		2	tablespoons rice wine or sherry

Sprinkle shrimp with lemon juice. Blend egg white and cornstarch; coat shrimp with mixture. heat oil in heavy, deep skillet or deep-fryer. Fry shrimp 2 to 3 minutes; remove with slotted spoon. Set aside; keep warm.

Break mushrooms into small pieces; cover with boiling water. Let soak 15 minutes. Drain bamboo shoots; reserve liquid. Cut shoots into thin strips.

Pour 2 tablespoons oil used for frying into skillet. Add bamboo shoots and onion; cook until transparent. Pour in 1/2 cup reserved liquid from bamboo shoots. Season with ground ginger. Add green pepper; cook 5 minutes (pepper should be crisp). Add curry powder, sugar, and soy sauce.

Drain soaked mushrooms. Add mushrooms, peas, and shrimp to skillet. Fold in carefully; heat through. Heat wine in small saucepan; pour over dish just before serving. Makes 4 servings.

Lime Spareribs

Mandarin Oranges with Shrimp

2	teaspoons sherry	¼	teaspoon sugar
1	teaspoon cornstarch	¼	teaspoon salt
½	pound shrimp, cleaned	**Boiled rice**	

Oil for cooking
½ cup drained canned mandarin-orange segments

Mix sherry and cornstarch together. Marinate shrimp in mixture 5 minutes.

Heat oil in wok or skillet, enough to cover bottom. Stir-fry shrimp just until color changes. Add mandarin-orange segments, sugar, and salt; stir-fry just until heated through, no more than 1 minute. Serve with rice. Makes 2 servings.

56/Fish and Seafood Main Courses

Shrimp and Asparagus

1 **pound cooked shrimp, shelled and deveined**	1½ **pounds fresh asparagus, steamed**
1 **can water chestnuts, drained and sliced**	2 **tablespoons oil**
1 **medium-sized onion, sliced**	¼ **teaspoon salt**
1 **cup fresh mushrooms, sliced**	½ **teaspoon freshly ground black pepper**
1 **cup celery, sliced diagonally**	2 **tablespoons sugar**
1 **small can mandarin oranges, drained**	2 **tablespoons soy sauce**
	Cooked rice

Prepare shrimp and set aside. Drain and slice water chestnuts. On a large tray, arrange shrimp, chestnuts, onion, mushrooms, celery, mandarin oranges, and asparagus. Heat oil in a wok. Add onion, celery, salt, pepper, and sugar. Stir-fry until vegetables are tender, but still on the crisp side. Add asparagus and shrimp.

Place water chestnuts and mushrooms over shrimp. Sprinkle with soy sauce and place orange sections on top. Cover and cook until mixture steams. Reduce heat and simmer about 10 minutes. Serve with rice. Makes 6 servings.

Shrimp with Peas

2 **quarts water**	**Salt to taste**
2 **cups frozen peas**	**Freshly ground black pepper to taste**
1 **tablespoon vegetable oil**	
1 **small slice fresh gingerroot**	1 **teaspoon cornstarch**
¼ **cup green onions, diagonally sliced**	1 **tablespoon cold water**
1 **cup uncooked shrimp, deveined, cut in half**	½ **teaspoon sesame-seed oil**

Bring water to boil. Add peas; bring to boil again. Drain peas; set aside.

Preheat wok (or skillet); coat bottom and sides with oil. Rub gingerroot on bottom and sides of wok, then discard. Stir-fry onions quickly. Add shrimp; stir-fry until just cooked. Shrimp will turn pink when done. Add salt and pepper.

Blend cornstarch with cold water. Stir this and peas into shrimp mixture. Add sesame oil; stir. Serve immediately. Makes 4 servings.

Deep-Fried Crispy Noodles

Hot-Mustard Shrimp

3	tablespoons powdered mustard	¾	cup flat beer
¼	teaspoon salt	1	pound shrimp, cleaned
1	teaspoon sugar	4	tablespoons melted butter
1	teaspoon horseradish	Duck sauce	

Mix mustard, salt, sugar, and horseradish together. Add enough beer to make a smooth paste. Gradually add rest of beer to make it thin. Let mixture stand for 1 hour. If it becomes too thick, add more beer or cold water.

Dip shrimp in mustard sauce; skewer and brush with melted butter. Grill on hibachi or grill for approximately 8 minutes. Turn frequently for an even browning. Serve with duck sauce. Makes 2 to 3 servings.

58/Fish and Seafood Main Courses

Shrimp Peking

1	**pound shrimp, cleaned and shelled**	2	**cloves garlic, minced**
½	**teaspoon salt**	2	**tablespoons soy sauce**
1	**egg, beaten**	2	**tablespoons chicken broth**
2	**tablespoons cornstarch**	1	**tablespoon dry sherry**
3	**tablespoons peanut oil**	2	**teaspoons red pepper, chopped**
2	**tablespoons scallions, finely chopped**	1	**tablespoon vinegar**
1	**small slice gingerroot, chopped**	2	**teaspoons sugar**
		4	**water chestnuts, sliced**

Sprinkle shrimp with salt. If shrimp are very large, cut in half. Mix together egg and cornstarch to make batter. Coat shrimp evenly with batter. Heat oil in wok (or frying pan) over medium-high heat. Stir-fry shrimp 3 minutes, separating them. Remove shrimp from wok. Drain; keep warm.

Place scallions and ginger in wok; stir-fry 1 minute. Add garlic, soy sauce, broth, sherry, red pepper, vinegar, and sugar. Cook, stirring constantly, until mixture comes to boil. Return shrimp to wok. Add water chestnuts; stir-fry 2 minutes. Serve immediately. Makes 2 servings.

Fried Shrimp with Pineapple

1	**cup all-purpose flour, sifted**	1	**pound raw shrimp, shelled and deveined**
1	**teaspoon baking powder**	1	**tablespoon cornstarch**
1	**teaspoon salt**	1	**tablespoon sugar**
1	**egg, beaten**	4	**tablespoons vinegar**
½	**cup beer**	½	**cup pineapple juice**
	Fat for deep frying	1	**cup pineapple chunks**

Sift flour, baking powder, and 1/2 teaspoon salt into bowl. Beat in egg and beer. Heat fat in deep-fryer or deep skillet to medium high. Dip shrimp in batter, coating well on all sides. Fry in hot fat until nicely browned. Drain; keep warm.

Mix cornstarch with sugar, 1/2 teaspoon salt, and vinegar. Add pineapple juice; cook over low heat, stirring constantly, until thickened.

Arrange shrimp on serving platter. Place pineapple chunks around shrimp; pour sauce over all. Makes 4 servings.

Fried Rice

Grilled Oriental Shrimp

1 pound shrimp, cleaned	1 tablespoon fresh gingerroot, finely chopped, or ¾ teaspoon powdered ginger
⅓ cup soy sauce	
¼ cup sesame oil	
1 tablespoon brown sugar	3 scallions, finely chopped

Combine all ingredients and marinate in refrigerator 6 hours. Drain shrimp, reserving marinade. Skewer shrimp and grill over a grill or hibachi approximately 5 minutes, turning frequently and basting with marinade. Makes 2 to 3 servings.

60/Fish and Seafood Main Courses

Fried Rice with Mushrooms

Shrimp and Bean Sprouts

1 cup celery, sliced diagonally	Oil for cooking
1 cup fresh mushrooms, sliced	½ pound fresh bean sprouts
½ cup scallions, sliced	½ pound cooked shrimp
	Soy sauce to taste

Prepare celery, mushrooms, and scallions. Heat oil in skillet or wok and stir-fry celery until it turns bright green. Add mushrooms and scallions and stir-fry for 1 minute. Add bean sprouts and shrimp and toss lightly until heated through, approximately 2 minutes. Sprinkle with soy sauce. Makes 2 servings.

Meat Main Courses

Beef in Oyster Sauce

½ teaspoon salt
¾ teaspoon baking soda
4 tablespoons water
3 teaspoons rice wine
½ teaspoon baking powder
¾ tablespoon cornstarch
2 teaspoons soy sauce
8 ounces lean beef, cut into bite-sized slices
3½ teaspoons oil

Oil for deep frying
6 scallions, cut into 2-inch slices
2 small slices fresh gingerroot
1½ teaspoons oyster sauce
¼ teaspoon MSG (optional)
¼ teaspoon sugar
½ teaspoon sesame oil
½ teaspoon cornstarch

Mix salt, baking soda, 3 tablespoons water, 1-1/2 teaspoons rice wine, baking powder, 3/4 tablespoon cornstarch, and 1 teaspoon soy sauce together. Coat beef slices with mixture. Add 1-1/2 teaspoons oil; let stand 1-1/2 hours.

Deep-fry beef in hot oil until color changes. Remove; drain on paper towels.

Sauté scallions and gingerroot in 2 tablespoons oil. Add beef, 1-1/2 teaspoons rice wine, oyster sauce, 1 teaspoon soy sauce, MSG, sugar, sesame oil, and cornstarch mixed with water. Stir-fry quickly until heated through. Makes 2 or 3 servings.

62/*Meat Main Courses*

Ginger Beef

1 cup onions, minced	8 fresh tomatoes, peeled and
2 cloves garlic, pressed	cut into large pieces
2 teaspoons turmeric	½ cup peanut oil
2 teaspoons ginger	4 cups beef bouillon
1 teaspoon chili powder	Boiled rice
1 teaspoon salt	Strips of red sweet pepper for
3 pounds of lean beef, cut	garnish
into cubes	

Combine onions, garlic, turmeric, ginger, chili powder, and salt in bowl. Mix well. Prepare beef and place in shallow dish. Sprinkle with onion-garlic mixture and refrigerate for 3 hours, stirring occasionally. Prepare tomatoes.

In large skillet, heat oil. Stir-fry the beef until browned on all sides. Place beef in casserole and add skillet drippings, tomatoes, and bouillon. Bake, covered, in 325°F oven for about 2 hours or until beef is tender. Serve with boiled rice and garnish with strips of red sweet pepper. Makes 6 to 8 servings.

Beef Slices Peking

3 tablespoons soy sauce	2 cloves garlic, minced
1 tablespoon sherry	½ teaspoon powdered ginger
1 pound lean beef, sliced	2 tablespoons soy sauce
paper-thin	⅛ teaspoon ground anise
1 cup oil	½ cup beef broth
2 tablespoons flour	1 teaspoon cornstarch
2 leeks, thinly sliced	

Blend soy sauce and sherry in a deep bowl. Add beef to marinade; coat well. Cover and let stand 1 hour.

Heat oil in large skillet. Thoroughly drain beef slices on paper towels. Sprinkle with flour. Add to hot oil; deep-fry 3 minutes. Remove meat with slotted spoon; drain. Set aside and keep warm.

Pour 4 tablespoons hot oil into another skillet. Throw away rest of frying oil. Reheat oil. Add leeks and garlic; cook 5 minutes, stirring. Add meat slices. Season with ginger, soy sauce, and anise. Pour in broth. Cover and simmer over very low heat 1 hour. At end of cooking time, bring to quick boil.

Blend cornstarch with small amount of cold water. Add to skillet; stir constantly until sauce is slightly thickened and bubbly. Correct seasoning, if necessary. Serve immediately. Makes 2 servings.

Meat Main Courses/63

Beef with Snow Peas

Marinade
1   teaspoon cornstarch
1   teaspoon soy sauce
2   teaspoons sherry
¼   teaspoon sugar
¼   teaspoon oil

Beef and Snow Peas
½   pound beef, thinly sliced
½   pound snow peas, with
     strings removed

2   teaspoons cornstarch
    mixed with 2 teaspoons
    cold water
⅛   teaspoon freshly ground
    black pepper
½   teaspoon sugar
¼   teaspoon MSG (optional)
2   tablespoons oil, divided
¼   teaspoon salt
1   teaspoon fresh gingerroot,
    grated
½   cup chicken stock

Mix marinade ingredients and marinate beef while preparing rest of ingredients.

String snow peas. Mix together cornstarch and water. Add pepper, sugar, and MSG. Heat skillet or wok to medium-high. Add 1 tablespoon oil, salt, and gingerroot. Add snow peas; stir. Add chicken stock. Cover for 10 seconds. Uncover, stir, and remove from pan.

Reheat pan and add remaining 1 tablespoon oil. When pan is hot, add beef and stir-fry only about 45 seconds, until beef is almost cooked. Then add snow peas and cornstarch mixture. Stir until sauce is thickened. Makes 2 to 3 servings.

Stir-Fried Beef and Mushrooms

½   pound dried Chinese
    mushrooms
¼   cup flour
1   tablespoon sugar
½   cup sherry
½   cup soy sauce
3   pounds lean steak, cut into
    thin strips

¾   cup oil
1   2-inch slice fresh
    gingerroot, minced
1   cup onions, chopped
2   cups beef bouillon
Salt to taste

Soak mushrooms in water 30 minutes. Drain well; set aside.

Combine flour, sugar, sherry, and soy sauce in bowl. Add steak; marinate 30 minutes, stirring frequently. Heat 1/2 cup oil in wok. Stir-fry gingerroot 1 minute. Add beef with marinade; stir-fry until beef changes color. Remove beef from wok.

Add remaining oil to wok. Add onions and stir-fry until almost tender. Add mushrooms and stir-fry until soft. Add beef to wok and stir-fry about 2 minutes. Add bouillon. Bring to boil; reduce heat. Add salt. Cover; cook 2 minutes. Makes 6 to 8 servings.

64/Meat Main Courses

Meat Platter Szechwan

7	tablespoons oil		Salt
6	ounces fresh mushrooms, sliced	¼	teaspoon ground ginger
½	pound tomatoes, peeled and sliced	½	pound onions, minced
		1	clove garlic, minced
		2	tablespoons sherry
½	pound green peppers, cut in half, seeds removed, and cut into julienne strips	1	cup hot beef broth (made from cubes)
		1	tablespoon soy sauce
1½	pounds lean pork, cut into 2-inch-long julienne strips	2	tablespoons cornstarch
		4	tablespoons water

Heat 4 tablespoons oil in skillet. Add mushrooms, tomatoes, and green peppers. Cook 5 minutes; set aside.

Heat 3 tablespoons oil in another skillet. Add meat strips. Season to taste with salt and ginger, stirring constantly. Brown 10 minutes. Add onions and garlic; cook 5 minutes. Pour in sherry. After 1 minute pour in broth and soy sauce. Add vegetable mixture. Cover; cook over medium heat 25 minutes.

Blend cornstarch with water; stir in. Cook until thickened and bubbly. Serve immediately on preheated platter. Makes 4 servings.

Marinated Steak Slices

1¼	pounds fillet steak, or sirloin	Salt to taste
4	tablespoons sherry	Pinch of sugar
4	tablespoons soy sauce	Pinch of white pepper
1½	heaping tablespoons cornstarch	4 tablespoons oil

Cut beef into thin slices. Prepare marinade by mixing the sherry, soy sauce, and cornstarch together thoroughly. Season with salt, sugar, and white pepper. Pour marinade over meat slices and let marinate for 1 hour.

In large skillet, heat oil until very hot. Pour in meat with marinade and cook for 5 minutes. Spoon into preheated bowl and serve with rice. Makes 2 to 3 servings.

Baked Chinese Cabbage

Marinated Flank Steak

1	flank steak, approximately 2 pounds

Marinade
- 4 tablespoons lemon juice
- ¼ cup soy sauce
- 3 tablespoons honey
- 3 scallions, finely chopped
- 2 tablespoons sesame oil

Score steak on each side. Combine marinade ingredients; place steak in mixture and refrigerate overnight, turning occasionally. Broil steak on preheated broiler pan about 4 minutes on each side, basting frequently with marinade. Cut steak on angle into very thin slices. Makes 2 to 3 servings.

66/Meat Main Courses

Oriental Meatballs

2 pounds lean ground beef	**3 tablespoons cornstarch**
2½ teaspoons salt	**2½ teaspoons soy sauce**
¼ teaspoon freshly ground black pepper	**½ cup vinegar**
1 egg, beaten	**½ cup light corn syrup**
2 tablespoons flour	**5 medium green peppers, cut into sixths**
Small amount freshly ground black pepper	**8 slices canned pineapple, quartered**
½ cup peanut oil	**10 maraschino cherries (optional)**
12 ounces canned chicken broth	

Combine beef, 1 teaspoon salt, and 1/4 teaspoon pepper. Shape into small meatballs. Combine egg, flour, 1/2 teaspoon salt, and small amount pepper. Beat until smooth. Heat oil and 1 teaspoon salt in large frying pan. Gently place meatballs in batter, 1 or 2 at a time; fry in hot oil, browning well on all sides. Remove meatballs from pan; drain remaining oil.

Blend 1/2 cup broth with cornstarch. Add remaining broth, soy sauce, vinegar, and corn syrup. Cook over medium heat, stirring constantly, until thick and clear. Add green peppers, pineapple, and cherries. Lower heat; cook slowly about 10 minutes. Pour over meatballs. Serve with rice. Makes 6 servings.

Marinated Lamb

3 pounds boneless lamb, cut into ½-inch cubes	**½ teaspoon saffron**
1 cup cider vinegar	**½ teaspoon dried ground chili peppers**
½ cup onions, minced	**1 teaspoon ground ginger**
3 cloves garlic, minced	**4 tablespoons oil**
2 teaspoons salt	**½ cup water**
1 teaspoon ground coriander	**Boiled rice**
1 teaspoon ground cumin	

Marinate lamb in vinegar 30 minutes; drain well. Grind onions, cloves, salt, coriander, cumin, saffron, chili peppers, and ginger together to make paste. Roll lamb in mixture and let stand 30 minutes.

Heat oil in pan. Brown lamb. Stir in water. Cover; cook over low heat 45 minutes or until lamb is very tender. Serve with rice. Makes 6 servings.

Spiced Beef

2 tablespoons peanut oil	1 teaspoon sugar
1 pound boneless stewing beef, cut into 1-inch cubes	3 scallions, cut into 1-inch pieces
2 tablespoons dry sherry	1 cup cold water
3 tablespoons soy sauce	¼ teaspoon star anise

Heat oil in skillet over high heat. Add beef; cook, turning constantly, until browned on all sides. Add sherry, soy sauce, and sugar; mix well. Cook 2 minutes. Stir in scallions.

Add water and bring to boil. Reduce heat to medium; cover. Cook 15 minutes, stirring occasionally. Stir in star anise. Reduce heat to low; cook 20 minutes. Makes 3 servings.

Braised Celery with Mushrooms

Chinese Cauliflower with Noodles

Lamb with Scallions

1	pound boneless lamb, fat trimmed, sliced ⅛ inch thick, and cut into strips	3	teaspoons cornstarch
		5	teaspoons soy sauce
		6	tablespoons sherry
½	teaspoon five-spice	2	tablespoons water
1	egg white	12	whole scallions
3	thin slices fresh gingerroot	2	tablespoons oil
3	cloves garlic, minced		

Mix lamb in bowl with five-spice, egg white, ginger, garlic, 1 teaspoon cornstarch, and 1 teaspoon soy sauce. Let stand 20 minutes. Blend rest of cornstarch, soy sauce, sherry, and water; set aside. Cut white part of scallions in half crosswise. Cut green tops into 1-inch pieces; set aside.

Heat oil in wok or skillet to high heat. Add meat mixture; cook, stirring constantly, until meat is slightly browned. Remove from wok.

Add cornstarch–soy-sauce mixture and white parts of onion to wok. Cook, stirring constantly, until thickened. Add meat and green tops of onions; stir until simmering. Makes 3 or 4 servings.

Meat Main Courses/69

Lamb with Garlic

2	pounds shoulder lamb chops	2	teaspoons whole anise pepper
Water for boiling		6	tablespoons soy sauce
16	cloves garlic	3	tablespoons sherry
1	leek, cut into 2-inch slices	Oil	
6	small slices fresh gingerroot	2	teaspoons cornstarch
2	cloves star anise	1	tablespoon water

Parboil lamb in enough water to cover; discard water. Place lamb, garlic, leek, ginger, star anise, whole anise pepper, soy sauce, and sherry in large pot with water to cover. Cover; bring to boil over high heat. Reduce heat to low; simmer until tender (about 1 hour). Remove lamb and drain liquid. Reserve liquid and garlic.

Heat oil to medium heat. Deep-fry lamb until crisp.

Heat 1 cup reserved liquid. Add cornstarch mixed with water; stir until thickened. Place lamb and garlic on serving platter; pour gravy over lamb. Makes 2 servings.

Honan Lamb Chops

2	tablespoons oil	1	pound fresh bean sprouts
4	shoulder lamb chops, about ¾ inch thick	½	teaspoon salt
1	medium-sized onion, diced	¼	teaspoon freshly ground black pepper
½	cup green pepper, diced	1½	teaspoons soy sauce
½	cup celery, diced	1	tablespoon cornstarch
1	can (approximately 5 ounces) bamboo shoots, sliced	1	tablespoon water
		1	medium-sized tomato, cut into wedges

Preheat wok or skillet to 350°F. Pour in oil. Add lamb; cook until browned on both sides. Add onion, green pepper, and celery. Drain bamboo shoots. Add liquid to wok. Cover; simmer on low heat about 30 minutes or until lamb is tender. Add sprouts, bamboo shoots, salt, and pepper.

Mix soy sauce, cornstarch, and water together until smooth. Stir into lamb mixture. Add tomato; cook 2 minutes, or until sauce has thickened. Makes 4 servings.

70/*Meat Main Courses*

Stir-Fried Lamb

1	tablespoon soy sauce	2	tablespoons peanut oil
1	teaspoon light brown sugar	2	teaspoons minced garlic
3	tablespoons chicken stock	Salt to taste	
1	tablespoon gin	3	leeks, white part only, sliced into 1-inch pieces
¼	teaspoon powdered five-spice		
1	pound boned lamb, cut into thin bite-sized pieces		

Mix soy sauce, sugar, stock, gin, and five-spice together. Marinate lamb in mixture 30 minutes.

Heat wok to high heat. Add oil, garlic, and salt; stir about 30 seconds or until garlic odor becomes strong. Add lamb and marinade; stir-fry 2 to 3 minutes. Add leeks; stir-fry 1 minute. Makes 3 or 4 servings.

Mandarin Liver

1	pound liver (pork, baby beef, or calves)	1	cup beef bouillon (from cubes)
2½	tablespoons flour	1	red pepper, cut into strips
5	tablespoons safflower oil	1	green pepper, cut into strips
Salt to taste		½	pound savoy cabbage, cut into strips
Pepper to taste		6	ounces fresh bean sprouts
3	tablespoons soy sauce	1	small can bamboo shoots (approximately 6 ounces)
2	tablespoons Chinese rice wine or sherry		
2	large onions, thinly sliced		

Pat liver dry with paper towels; cut into thin slices. Coat with flour. Heat oil in heavy skillet. Add liver; brown on all sides; remove. Season to taste with salt and pepper. Set aside; keep warm.

Add soy sauce, wine, and onions to pan drippings; simmer 5 minutes. Pour in beef bouillon. Add red and green peppers and cabbage; simmer 10 minutes. Vegetables should still be crisp. Add bean sprouts, bamboo shoots, and liver; heat through. Serve immediately. Makes 4 servings.

Mixed Chinese Vegetables

72/Meat Main Courses

Pork with Peas

Marinade
2	tablespoons soy sauce
2	teaspoons rice wine or sherry
⅛	teaspoon MSG (optional)
1	egg white
1	teaspoon cornstarch

Salt
White pepper

12	ounces lean pork, cut crosswise into thin strips
4	ounces frozen peas
8	tablespoons oil
½	cup hot beef broth (made from cubes)

Salt

Sugar
1	leek, cut into julienne strips
1	clove garlic, minced
4	ounces canned sliced mushrooms
4	ounces canned bamboo shoots
1	preserved gingo plum, sliced
1	tablespoon rice wine or sherry
1	tablespoon cornstarch
2	teaspoons soy sauce
2	tablespoons oyster sauce

White pepper
Pinch of ground ginger

Make marinade by thoroughly combining soy sauce, wine, MSG, egg white, and cornstarch. Season to taste with salt and white pepper. Pour marinade over pork; cover. Let marinate 30 minutes.

Meanwhile, thaw peas. Heat 2 tablespoons oil in small saucepan. Add peas; pour in broth. Season to taste with salt and sugar; cook 5 minutes. Drain peas, reserving cooking liquid; keep warm.

Heat 3 tablespoons oil in large saucepan. Add leek, garlic, mushrooms, bamboo shoots, and gingo plum. Cook 5 minutes, stirring constantly. Set aside; keep warm.

Heat 3 tablespoons oil in skillet. Add meat with marinade; cook 3 minutes or until meat is browned, stirring occasionally. Add meat and peas to large saucepan with vegetables. Pour in wine and reserved cooking liquid; bring to boil.

Blend cornstarch with soy sauce and oyster sauce; stir until slightly thickened and bubbly. Season to taste with salt, pepper, ginger, and sugar. Serve immediately. Makes 2 servings.

Slow Roast Spareribs

3 to 4 pounds pork spareribs
Salt and pepper

1 level teaspoon dried rosemary

Wipe pork and put it in a roasting pan. Sprinkle liberally with salt, a little pepper, and rosemary. Roast in a 300°F oven for 1-1/2 to 2 hours. Cut pork into individual ribs and serve hot. Makes 4 servings.

Red and Green Pepper Pot

Spicy Pork

- 1½ pounds lean pork
- 3 tablespoons peanut oil
- 3 cloves garlic, minced
- 2 small slices fresh gingerroot, minced
- ½ cup leek, cut into 2-inch pieces
- ½ cup bamboo shoots, sliced
- ½ cup small pieces red or green sweet pepper
- ¼ teaspoon crushed red pepper
- 3 tablespoons water
- 1½ teaspoons sugar
- 4 tablespoons hoisin sauce
- Boiled rice

Boil pork 25 minutes; cool. Slice into bite-sized pieces; set aside.

Heat oil in wok or skillet over high heat. Cook garlic and ginger 1 minute. Add leek, bamboo shoots, and sweet pepper; mix well. Stir in red pepper. Add pork slices; mix through. Add water; bring to boil. Add sugar and hoisin sauce; stir quickly 1 minute or until sauce coats ingredients. Serve with rice. Makes 4 servings.

74/Meat Main Courses

Chop Suey

1	pound lean pork, cut into thin slices	8	tablespoons oil
2	tablespoons sherry	2	medium-sized onions, thinly sliced
2	tablespoons soy sauce	¼	cup bamboo shoots, thinly sliced
Salt to taste		1	cup fresh bean sprouts
Freshly ground pepper to taste		½	pound fresh mushrooms, sliced
Pinch of powdered ginger		3	tablespoons soy sauce
2	ounces transparent noodles, broken into small pieces	1	teaspoon sugar
		⅛	teaspoon MSG (optional)
1	stalk celery, cut into thin slices	1	tablespoon cornstarch
		2	jiggers sherry
4	tablespoons dried Chinese mushrooms, soaked in water for 30 minutes	Cooked rice	

Cut pork into thin slices and mix with 2 tablespoons sherry, 2 tablespoons soy sauce, salt, pepper, and ginger. Place in glass or ceramic bowl. Press down meat and cover. Let marinate for 1 hour. Break noodles into small pieces and boil in salted water for 5 minutes. Drain and set aside. Cut celery in thin slices; blanch for 5 minutes. Drain and set aside. Slice Chinese mushrooms into bite-sized pieces.

Heat oil in skillet until very hot. Add marinated pork and fry for 2 minutes. Remove and keep warm. Add onions, bamboo shoots, bean sprouts, and fresh mushrooms. Simmer for 3 minutes. Fold in meat, celery, and noodles. Season with 3 tablespoons soy sauce, sugar, and MSG. Stirring carefully, cook for an additional 3 minutes.

Blend cornstarch with 2 jiggers sherry and slowly stir into sauce until sauce is thick and bubbly. Correct seasonings if necessary and serve immediately with rice. Makes approximately 3 servings.

Bean Curd with Pork

½	pound ground pork	2	tablespoons scallions, chopped
3	tablespoons soy sauce		
1	tablespoon hoisin sauce	1	tablespoon oil
1	teaspoon Tabasco sauce	½	cup green peppers, diced
2	tablespoons cornstarch	4	pieces bean curd
¼	teaspoon sesame-seed oil		

Mix pork with soy sauce, hoisin sauce, Tabasco sauce, cornstarch, and sesame-seed oil. Quickly fry scallions in 1 tablespoon oil. Add pork mixture, green pepper, and bean curd. Stir-fry 10 to 15 minutes or until pork is done. Makes 4 servings.

Meat Main Courses/75

Cantonese Pork Roast

1 (2½- to 3-pound) boneless pork roast	1 tablespoon sugar
1 tablespoon soy sauce	Salt to taste
2 tablespoons chicken broth	2 tablespoons sesame-seed oil
1 tablespoon honey	

Rinse pork and pat dry with paper towels. Blend next five ingredients and spoon over meat and rub in thoroughly. Place roast in bowl, cover, and let stand for 1 hour. Remove and drain, reserving any marinade.

Brush meat with oil and place in ovenproof dish. Brush with reserved marinade. Place in preheated 325°F oven and roast for approximately 1-1/2 hours. Makes 4 to 6 servings.

Sweet-and-Sour Yams and Pineapple

76/Meat Main Courses

Vegetables with Pork

¼	cup butter	1¼	cups beef bouillon
4	cups celery, sliced diagonally	1	tablespoon cornstarch
1	green sweet pepper, sliced	3	tablespoons soy sauce
1	red sweet pepper, sliced	½	teaspoon powdered ginger
½	pound fresh mushrooms, sliced	¼	teaspoon salt
½	cup onions, sliced		Freshly ground pepper to taste
2	cups cooked pork, cubed		Boiled rice

Melt butter in a wok. Add celery and stir-fry for 5 minutes. Stir in the green and red pepper, mushrooms, and onions and stir-fry for another 5 minutes. Stir in pork and beef bouillon and bring to a boil. Reduce heat and simmer for 5 minutes.

Blend cornstarch with the soy sauce, ginger, salt, and pepper. Stir into the pork mixture. Cook, stirring constantly, just until heated through and thickened. Serve over rice. Makes 6 servings.

Lime Spareribs

4	pounds spareribs, cut into serving pieces	¼	cup lime juice
¼	cup olive oil	2	tablespoons prepared mustard
1	cup onions, chopped	¼	cup soy sauce
1	cup fresh mushrooms, sliced	⅔	cup water
1	clove garlic, minced	2	tablespoons honey
½	cup chili sauce	1	teaspoon salt
2	tablespoons red wine vinegar		Freshly ground pepper to taste

Cut spareribs into serving pieces and place in baking pan. Heat oil in saucepan. Sauté onions, mushrooms, and garlic until tender. Add chili sauce, vinegar, lime juice, mustard, soy sauce, water, honey, salt, and pepper; mix thoroughly. Pour sauce over the spareribs.

Bake in a 325°F oven for 1 hour, or until the spareribs are tender. Baste frequently. Makes 6 to 8 servings.

Meat Main Courses/77

Sweet-and-Sour Pork

1½ **pounds lean pork, cut in 1-inch cubes**	1 **small slice fresh gingerroot, minced**
3 **tablespoons soy sauce**	½ **cup onions, chopped**
3 **tablespoons dry white wine**	¼ **pound fresh mushrooms, sliced**
2 **carrots, cut into thin strips**	½ **cup beef broth**
1 **red sweet pepper, seeds removed and cut into thin rings**	1 **recipe Sweet-and-Sour Sauce (see Index)**
4 **tablespoons olive oil, divided**	**Boiled rice**

Place pork in shallow dish. Combine soy sauce and wine and pour over pork. Turn to coat all sides. Marinate for about 20 to 30 minutes, stirring frequently. Cut carrots and set aside. Cut pepper into rings and set aside.

Heat 2 tablespoons of the oil in a wok and add gingerroot. Place the pork in the wok and stir-fry for about 5 minutes. Remove pork and set aside. Add remaining oil to wok. Add carrots, sweet pepper, onions, and mushrooms and stir-fry for about 5 minutes or until the carrots and sweet pepper are tender but still on the crisp side. Add pork and stir-fry for 5 minutes longer. Add broth and mix well.

Stir in the sweet-and-sour sauce and bring to a boil. Reduce heat to low, cover wok, and cook for 2 minutes longer. Serve with rice. Makes 4 servings.

Rice and Noodles

Deep-Fried Crispy Noodles

1 **(5-ounce) package fine egg noodles**	**Vegetable oil**

Place noodles in large saucepan in enough water to cover; bring to boil. Cook, stirring occasionally, 5 minutes; drain well.

Fill deep-fat fryer half full with oil; heat to 350°F. Drop noodles into basket in oil; cook 2 minutes. Remove from oil; drain well on paper towels.

Heat oil to 375°F. Return noodles to fryer; cook until golden brown and crisp. Drain well on paper towels; separate noodles if necessary. Makes 4 to 5 cups noodles.

Soft-Fried Noodles with Mushrooms

1 **(5-ounce) package fine egg noodles**	1 **cup almonds, sliced**
2 **tablespoons safflower oil**	½ **cup chicken broth**
1 **cup bamboo shoots**	3 **tablespoons soy sauce**
1 **cup fresh mushrooms, sliced**	**Salt to taste**

Cook noodles in large pot in boiling, lightly salted water 8 minutes; drain well.

Heat oil in wok or skillet over low heat. Add noodles; stir-fry 4 minutes. Stir in bamboo shoots, mushrooms, and almonds; mix thoroughly. Stir in broth, soy sauce, and salt. Reduce heat to low; simmer, covered, 20 minutes or until liquid is almost absorbed. Makes 8 servings.

Chinese Almond Cookies

"Sizzling" Rice

1 cup long-grain rice	**2 teaspoons salt**
4 cups water	**Oil for deep frying**

At least a day in advance, combine rice, water, and salt in 2-quart saucepan. Let stand 30 minutes. Bring to boil; cover. Simmer 30 minutes; drain. Spread evenly on heavily greased cookie sheet. Bake in 250°F oven 8 hours, turning occasionally with spatula. Break crusty rice into bite-sized pieces. These can be stored in airtight containers in refrigerator several weeks.

Just before serving time, heat oven to 250°F; warm serving platter. Pour oil about 2 inches deep in 6-quart saucepan (or deep-fryer). Heat to 425°F. Fry rice, stirring with slotted spoon, until golden brown, approximately 5 minutes. Drain quickly; place in warmed serving platter. Makes 5 or 6 servings.

80/Rice and Noodles

Fried Rice

½ **pound long-grain rice**	3 **tablespoons oil**
½ **pound cooked ham, cut into strips**	2 **tablespoons soy sauce**
	1 **leek, sliced**
1 **(6-ounce) can shrimp, drained**	4 **eggs**
	Freshly ground black pepper

Cook rice according to package directions. Cut ham into strips. Drain shrimp.

Heat oil in large skillet. Add ham and shrimp and cook until lightly browned, approximately 5 minutes. Add rice and soy sauce. Cook another 5 minutes. Add leek and cook for an additional 5 minutes, stirring occasionally. Lightly beat eggs with pepper. Pour over rice and cook until eggs are set. Serve on preheated platter. Makes 4 servings.

Fried Rice with Mushrooms

½ **cup dried mushrooms, sliced**	1 **tablespoon soy sauce**
¼ **cup olive oil**	½ **cup white bean curd, cut into cubes**
¼ **cup green onions, sliced**	¼ **cup safflower oil**
2 **cups long-grain rice**	¾ **cup cooked fresh green peas**
4 **cups chicken stock**	
⅛ **teaspoon dry mustard**	**Radish flowers for garnish**

Soak mushrooms in cold water 5 minutes; drain well.

Heat olive oil in wok or deep skillet over medium heat. Add onions; stir-fry until onions are limp and transparent. Add rice; stir-fry until rice is golden. Add 1 cup stock and mustard; stir-fry 2 to 3 minutes or until liquid is absorbed. Add 1 cup stock and soy sauce; stir-fry until liquid is absorbed. Add 1 cup stock; reduce heat to low. Stir in bean curd; cook, stirring occasionally, until liquid is absorbed.

Add remaining stock, safflower oil, peas, and mushrooms. Cover; cook, stirring occasionally, about 20 to 25 minutes or until rice is tender. Spoon into serving dish; garnish with radish flowers. Makes 10 servings.

Pear and Ginger Preserve

Vegetables

Baked Chinese Cabbage

2 heads Chinese cabbage
4 cups beef bouillon
1 small onion, coarsely
  chopped
Margarine to grease ovenproof
  baking dish
6 tablespoons Emmenthal or
  Gruyère cheese, grated
2 tablespoons butter or
  margarine

Sauce
½ cup sour cream
2 tablespoons parsley,
  chopped
1 small onion, chopped
Salt to taste
White pepper to taste
1½ tablespoons Emmenthal or
  Gruyère cheese, grated

Remove outer wilted leaves from cabbage and cut cabbage in half lengthwise. Cut each half into 3 or 4 pieces. Wash thoroughly and pat dry. Bring beef bouillon to boil, add onion and cabbage, and simmer for 20 minutes. Remove cabbage with slotted spoon and drain.

Grease ovenproof baking dish with margarine. Place 1/3 of cabbage in dish, sprinkle with 1/3 of cheese, and dot with 1/3 of butter or margarine. Repeat this until cabbage, cheese, and butter are used.

Prepare sauce by combining and stirring thoroughly sour cream, parsley, onion, salt, and pepper. Pour over cabbage. Sprinkle with 1-1/2 tablespoons grated cheese. Bake in preheated 375°F oven until cheese melts completely, approximately 10 to 15 minutes. Makes approximately 4 servings.

Braised Celery with Mushrooms

- 1 bunch celery
- 1 cup chicken stock or water and chicken stock cubes
- ¼ pound mushrooms
- 4 tablespoons margarine
- 2 tablespoons flour
- ½ cup milk
- 2 tablespoons Cheddar cheese, grated

Scrub celery until very clean. Put stock in a saucepan, bring to a boil. Add celery and cook for 20 to 25 minutes or until very tender. Drain celery and put in an ovenproof dish. Reserve stock.

Slice mushrooms, fry in 1/2 of the margarine. Drain well. Scatter mushrooms over celery.

Melt remaining margarine in a saucepan, stir in flour, and cook gently for 2 to 3 minutes. Add milk and 1/2 cup of reserved stock. Bring to a boil, stirring, then simmer for 2 to 3 minutes. Pour sauce over vegetables and sprinkle with cheese. Broil in a hot oven just until bubbling. Serve hot. Makes 4 servings.

Chinese Fruit Salad

84/Vegetables

Chinese Cauliflower with Noodles

1 **small head of cauliflower**	2 **tablespoons soy sauce**
2 **tablespoons oil, divided**	1 **cup beef bouillon**
½ **pound beef, thinly sliced**	1 **teaspoon cornstarch**
Salt to taste	½ **teaspoon cold water**
1 **small onion, chopped**	½ **pound egg noodles**

Clean cauliflower and divide into small florets. Heat 1 tablespoon oil in heavy skillet. Add cauliflower and beef slices and cook until lightly browned. Season with salt. Add chopped onion and soy sauce and cook for 5 minutes. Pour in beef bouillon and simmer for 35 minutes. Blend cornstarch with cold water. Stir into cauliflower mixture until slightly thick and bubbly.

Cook egg noodles in 3 quarts of salted water for 10 minutes. Drain. Heat other tablespoon of oil in skillet, add noodles, and fry until golden. Mix noodles with cauliflower. Heat through and serve. Makes 4 servings.

Sweet-and-Sour Yams and Pineapple

1 **(20-ounce) can sliced pineapple; drain and reserve syrup**	**Oil**
	4 **scallions, sliced**
1 **tablespoon cornstarch**	1 **small green pepper, cut into small chunks**
¼ **teaspoon salt**	½ **cup celery, sliced diagonally**
3 **tablespoons fresh lemon juice**	
2 **(1-pound) cans of yams, drained**	

Drain pineapple; reserve syrup. In saucepan, combine reserved syrup, cornstarch, and salt. Blend well. Bring to a boil over medium heat. Cook until thickened, stirring constantly. Stir in lemon juice.

Arrange pineapple and yams in casserole and pour sauce over mixture. Bake, covered, in a 350°F oven for about 30 minutes or until hot.

In small amount of oil in skillet, sauté scallions, green pepper chunks, and celery until just tender, but still crisp. Stir carefully into yam mixture. Serve immediately. Makes approximately 8 servings.

Pickled Figs

Red and Green Pepper Pot

- ¼ cup butter
- 3 red peppers, cut into rings
- 3 green peppers, cut into rings
- 6 yellow onions, peeled and cut into wedges
- 12 tomatoes, stem ends cut off, cut into wedges
- Salt to taste
- Freshly ground black pepper to taste

Melt butter in skillet. Add peppers and onions; sauté over low heat 10 minutes, stirring frequently. Add tomato wedges. Season with salt and pepper. Cook 10 minutes, stirring frequently. Makes 6 servings.

Spiced Mandarin Oranges

Mixed Chinese Vegetables

5	large dried Chinese mushrooms	4	tablespoons sesame-seed oil
1	cup lukewarm water	2	ounces frozen peas
5	ounces green cabbage	½	cup hot chicken broth
4	ounces carrots	2	tablespoons soy sauce
4	ounces cucumber		Salt
5	ounces canned bamboo shoots		Pinch of sugar
			Pinch of MSG (optional)

Soak mushrooms in water for 30 minutes. Shred cabbage; cut carrots, cucumber, and bamboo shoots into julienne strips. Cube mushrooms.

Heat oil in skillet. Add cabbage and cook for 2 minutes. Add mushrooms, cucumbers, carrots, bamboo shoots, and peas. Pour in chicken broth. Season with soy sauce, salt, sugar, and MSG. Simmer over low heat for 15 minutes. Serve immediately. Makes 2 servings.

Desserts

Almond Delight

1	envelope unflavored gelatin	
3	tablespoons warm water	
1	small can evaporated milk	
1¼	cups cold water	
6	tablespoons sugar	
1	tablespoon almond extract	
1	small can mandarin oranges (drain; reserve juice)	

Orange Syrup
- ¼ cup sugar
- 2 cups warm water
- 1 teaspoon almond extract
- Juice from mandarin oranges

Dissolve gelatin in warm water. Heat milk with cold water and sugar to just below boiling. Add gelatin mixture; cool. Add almond extract. Pour into square or rectangular glass dish; refrigerate to set. Cut into squares; float in syrup with mandarin oranges.

To make orange syrup, dissolve sugar in water. Add almond extract and juice. Chill before serving. Serve in rice bowls. Makes 4 servings.

88/Desserts

Chinese Almond Cookies

¼ pound margarine	Pinch of salt
1 cup granulated sugar	Blanched almonds for
1 egg, beaten	decoration
1 teaspoon almond essence	Little milk for glazing
3 cups flour	
2 level teaspoons baking powder	

Grease 2 baking trays. In a large bowl, cream margarine and sugar together with a wooden spoon until mixture is light and fluffy. Gradually beat in egg and almond essence a little at a time. Sift flour, baking powder, and salt, then stir into egg mixture. Form mixture into 1- to 1-1/2-inch balls with wet hands and place on greased baking trays.

Split almonds in half length-wise and place 1/2 on each cookie, pressing down slightly at the same time to flatten each one. Brush with a little milk, then bake at 350°F oven for 20 minutes or until golden. Remove from baking trays and cool on a wire rack. Makes 36 to 48 cookies.

Chinese Fruit Salad

1 (4-ounce) jar ginger in syrup, drained	1 (16-ounce) can mangos, drained
1 (11-ounce) can lichees in syrup, drained	1 round watermelon, chilled, cut in half, meat and seeds removed, meat cut into balls or cubes
1 (8-ounce) can kumquats, drained	
1 (20-ounce) can longans, drained	1 (18-ounce) can white nuts
1 (12-ounce) can water-lily roots, drained	1 lemon, sliced

Place ginger, lichees, kumquats, longans, lily roots, and mangos in large bowl; mix well. Chill until cold.

Cut slice off base of each watermelon half; place each half on serving dish. Place melon balls or cubes back into shells. Spoon mixed fruit on watermelon balls. Serve with nuts and lemon. Makes about 12 servings.

Note: All the fruits in this recipe are available at Oriental food stores.

Honey Shortbread

Almond Triangles

½ cup butter	½ teaspoon salt
1 cup sugar	2 cups flour
6 tablespoons whipping cream	Chopped almonds
3 eggs	

Combine butter and sugar in bowl; cream together until smooth. Beat in whipping cream and 2 eggs. Add salt and flour; blend well. Wrap in waxed paper; chill overnight.

Roll out dough on lightly floured surface; cut into triangles.

Beat remaining egg slightly; brush over top surfaces of triangles. Sprinkle with almonds. Place on greased baking sheet. Bake in preheated 375°F oven 8 to 10 minutes or until golden brown. Makes 3 to 4 dozen cookies.

90/Desserts

Honey Shortbread

2½ cups all-purpose flour **½ cup butter**
Pinch of salt **½ cup honey**

In medium-sized bowl, place flour and salt. Mix butter into flour with your fingers until mixture is like fine meal. Add honey gradually and, still working with your fingers, blend until dough is smooth and leaves the side of the bowl. From a piece of cardboard, cut a fan-shaped pattern.

Roll out the dough on lightly floured surface to about 1/4 inch thick and cut into fan shapes. Place on baking sheet that has been lightly floured and cut 6 deep slashes lengthwise as shown in picture. Bake in preheated 350°F oven until lightly browned, about 12 minutes. Makes approximately 2-1/2 dozen "fans."

Pickled Figs

5 quarts firm ripe figs
1 cup soda
4 to 5 cups sugar
2½ cups vinegar
1 teaspoon salt
¼ teaspoon ground nutmeg
2 teaspoons whole cloves

2 teaspoons whole allspice
1 medium piece fresh
gingerroot
3 sticks cinnamon
Green food coloring
(optional)

Place figs in large bowl; sprinkle with soda. Add 6 quarts boiling water; let stand 5 minutes. Rinse figs thoroughly in cool water; drain.

Combine 2-1/2 cups sugar and 2 quarts water in kettle; bring to boil. Add figs; cook 30 minutes or until tender. Add remaining sugar, vinegar, salt, and nutmeg.

Tie whole spices in bag; drop into syrup. Cook until figs are clear. Let stand in cool place overnight. Add coloring if desired. Pack figs to within 1/2 inch of top of pint jars.

Bring syrup to boil; pour over figs. Place lids on jars; screw bands tight. Process 15 minutes in boiling water. Makes about 6 pints.

Almond Triangles

Spiced Mandarin Oranges

1	small tangerine (an orange may be substituted)
2	(11-ounce) cans mandarin oranges
¼	cup water
⅓	cup brown sugar, firmly packed
1	2-inch piece of stick cinnamon

Cut the peeling from the tangerine in paper-thin strips. Squeeze the juice and strain.

In medium-sized saucepan, combine the peeling and juice with the rest of the ingredients. Simmer for 15 minutes. Remove from heat and remove the peeling and cinnamon. Chill for several hours. Serve in small dessert dishes. Makes about 4 servings.

92/Desserts

Pear and Ginger Preserve

2	pounds prepared pears (about 6)	2	cups white sugar
2	tablespoons lemon juice	1	cup water
6	cloves	4	tablespoons preserved ginger (in syrup)

Peel, core, and cut pears into 1/2-inch pieces. Put them in a bowl and mix in lemon juice and cloves. Place sugar in a saucepan, add water, and bring to a boil, stirring until sugar is dissolved. Boil, uncovered, for 8 minutes. Add pear mixture to syrup, bring to a boil again, and boil gently until pears are tender and liquid very syrupy.

Finely chop ginger and stir it into the preserve. Bring to a boil again, then put aside to cool slightly. Skim if necessary. Pour hot preserve into hot clean jars. Leave until completely cold before covering the jars. Makes about 4 pints.

Caramel Apples

4	dessert apples, cored and quartered		Oil for deep-frying
3	tablespoons flour	1	cup granulated sugar
1	tablespoon cornstarch	2	tablespoons oil
2	egg whites	2	tablespoons sesame seeds

Dust apple quarters with a little flour. Sift remaining flour with cornstarch into a bowl. Add egg whites and beat well with a wooden spoon to form a smooth batter. Coat apple quarters in batter.

Fill a wok 1/3 to 1/2 full of oil and heat it until a bread cube will brown quickly. Deep-fry apple quarters for about 5 minutes or until golden brown; drain on paper towels.

Place sugar in wok with 4 tablespoons water; stir until sugar has dissolved. Add oil and heat, without stirring, to allow the sugar to caramelize and turn golden brown. Stir in apple and sesame seeds and coat them well. Serve immediately. Makes 4 servings.

Caramel Apples

EQUIVALENT MEASURES

dash = 2 or 3 drops
pinch = amount that can be held
        between ends of thumb &
        forefinger
1 tablespoon = 3 teaspoons
¼ cup = 4 tablespoons
⅓ cup = 5 tablespoons + 1 teaspoon
½ cup = 8 tablespoons
1 cup = 16 tablespoons
1 pint = 2 cups
1 quart = 4 cups
1 gallon = 4 quarts
1 peck = 8 quarts
1 bushel = 4 pecks
1 pound = 16 ounces

KITCHEN METRIC

measurements you will encounter
most often in recipes are: centimeter
(cm), milliliter (ml), gram (g),
kilogram (kg)

cup equivalents (volume):

  ¼ cup = 60 ml
  ⅓ cup = 85 ml
  ½ cup = 125 ml
  ⅔ cup = 170 ml
  ¾ cup = 180 ml
  1 cup = 250 ml
  1¼ cups = 310 ml
  1½ cups = 375 ml
  2 cups = 500 ml
  3 cups = 750 ml
  5 cups = 1250 ml

spoonful equivalents (volume):

  ⅛ teaspoon = .5 ml
  ¼ teaspoon = 1.5 ml
  ½ teaspoon = 3 ml
  ¾ teaspoon = 4 ml
  1 teaspoon = 5 ml
  1 tablespoon = 15 ml
  2 tablespoons = 30 ml
  3 tablespoons = 45 ml

pan sizes (linear & volume):

  1 inch = 2.5 cm
  8-inch square = 20-cm square
  9 × 13 × 1½-inch = 20 × 33 × 4-cm

10 × 6 × 2-inch = 25 × 15 × 5-cm
13 × 9 × 2-inch = 33 × 23 × 5-cm
7½ × 12 × 1½-inch = 18 × 30 × 4-cm
  (above are baking dishes, pans)
9 × 5 × 3-inch = 23 × 13 × 8-cm
  (loaf pan)
10-inch = 25 cm 12-inch = 30-cm
  (skillets)
1-quart = 1-liter 2-quart = 2-liter
  (baking dishes, by volume)
5- to 6-cup = 1.5-liter
  (ring mold)

weight (meat amounts;
  can & package sizes):

1 ounce = 28 g
½ pound = 225 g
¾ pound = 340 g
1 pound = 450 g
1½ pounds = 675 g
2 pounds = 900 g
3 pounds = 1.4 kg (in recipes,
  amounts of meat above 2 pounds
  will generally be stated in
  kilograms)
10 ounces = 280 g
  (most frozen vegetables)
10½ ounces = 294 g
  (most condensed soups)
15 ounces = 425 g
  (common can size)
16 ounces = 450 g
  (common can size)
1 pound, 24 ounces = 850 g
  (can size)

OVEN TEMPERATURES

275°F = 135°C
300°F = 149°C
325°F = 165°C
350°F = 175°C
375°F = 190°C
400°F = 205°C
425°F = 218°C
450°F = 230°C
500°F = 260°C

Note that Celsius temperatures are
sometimes rounded off to the nearest
reading ending in 0 or 5; the Celsius
thermometer is the same as
Centigrade, a term no longer used.

Index

Almond Delight, 87
Apples, Caramel, 92
Asparagus, Shrimp and, 56

Bean Curd with Pork, 74
Beef
  Flank Steak, Marinated, 65
  Ginger, 62
  in Oyster Sauce, 61
  Slices Peking, 62
  with Snow Peas, 63
  Spiced, 67
  Steak Slices, Marinated, 64
  Stir-Fried and Mushrooms, 63
Beef, Ground
  Dumplings, Soup with Vegetables
    and Meat, 22
  Meatballs, Cocktail, 11
  Meatballs, Oriental, 66

Cabbage, Baked Chinese, 82
Caramel Apples, 92
Cauliflower, Chinese with Noodles, 84
Celery, Braised with Mushrooms, 83
Chicken
  Balls in Oyster Sauce, 32
  Barbecued, 28
  Cantonese, 26
  Cashew, 30
  Chow Mein, 28
  with Dates, 30
  Deep-Fried Sweet-and-Sour, 37
  Kang Pao, 33
  Lemon, 31

  with Mandarin Oranges and
    Almonds, 40
  Oriental, 33
  Paper-Wrapped, 40
  with Pineapple, 38
  Roast, 34
  Salad, Honan-Style, 13
  Sesame, 34
  Soup, Vegetable, 22
  Soup, Velvet, 16
  with Sweet Peppers, 36
  Sweet-and-Sour Barbecued, 39
  with Vegetables, 37
  Velvet, 38
  with Walnuts, 36
  Wings, 6
  Wings, Crusty-Crumbed, 6
  Wings in Oyster Sauce, 6
Chop Suey, 74
Cookies
  Almond Triangles, 89
  Chinese Almond, 88
  Honey Shortbread, 90
Crab Soup, 21
Cucumber Hors d'Oeuvres, 7

Duck
  Chinese, 44
  Crispy, 45
  Peking, 42
  Pineapple, 41
  Szechwan, 46

Egg Rolls, 8

Figs, Pickled, 90
Fish
 Chinese, 50
 Poached, Mandarin-Style, 50
 Steamed Whole, 52
 in Sweet-and-Sour Sauce, 52
Fruit Salad, Chinese, 88
Halibut Cantonese, 48

Lamb
 Chops, Honan, 69
 with Garlic, 69
 Marinated, 66
 with Scallions, 68
 Stir-Fried, 70
Liver Mandarin, 70

Mandarin Oranges, Spiced, 91
Meat Platter Szechwan, 64

Noodles
 Chinese Cauliflower with, 84
 Deep-Fried Crispy, 78
 Soft-Fried with Mushrooms, 78

Oysters in Ginger Sauce, 54

Pancakes, Mandarin, 43
Pear and Ginger Preserve, 92
Pepper Pot, Red and Green, 85
Pineapple Cocktail Barbecue, 10
Pork
 Bean Curd with, 74
 with Peas, 72
 Roast, Cantonese, 75
 Spareribs in Honey Sauce, 11
 Spareribs, Lime, 76
 Spareribs, Slow Roast, 72
 Spareribs, Sweet-and-Sour, 5
 Spicy, 73
 Sweet-and-Sour, 77
 Vegetables with, 76

Rice
 "Sizzling," 79
 Fried, 80
 Fried with Mushrooms, 80

Salad
 Chicken, Honan-Style, 13
 Chinese Fruit, 88
 Fruited Rice, 16
 Lychee and Sesame, 14
 Mandarin, 16
 Mandarin-Orange, 14
Salmon, Sesame, 51
Sauce
 Sweet-and-Sour Plum, 11
 Sweet-and-Sour, 12
Scallops Honan-Style, 10
Shrimp
 and Asparagus, 56
 and Bean Sprouts, 60
 Curried, 54
 Fried with Pineapple, 58
 Grilled Oriental, 59
 Hot-Mustard, 57
 Mandarin Oranges with, 55
 with Peas, 56
 Peking, 58
 Toast, 10
Soup
 Black-Mushroom, 19
 Celery, 20
 Chicken Vegetable, 22
 Chicken Velvet, 16
 Crab, 21
 Egg Drop, 17
 Hot-and-Sour, 18
 Mandarin, 18
 Noodle, 24
 Shark's-Fin, 20
 with Vegetables and Meat
  Dumplings, 22
 Wonton, 24

Vegetables, Mixed Chinese, 86

Wontons, 9

Yams, Sweet-and-Sour and Pineapple,
 84